NIAGARA STORY

VOLUME I

BEGINNINGS

BY

ROBERT J. FOLEY

ILLUSTRATED BY

GEORGE BALBAR

To Bob
Merry Christmas 1994
Best of... George Balbar

THE HAUNTED PRESS

NIAGARA FALLS, ONTARIO

ISBN: 1-895528-00-3

First Printing - April, 1994

Second Printing - November, 1994

Foley, Robert J. 1941-

Niagara Story Volume I

by Robert J. Foley

Includes index

Illustrated by

Balbar, George

Printed in Canada by: Peninsula Press Limited, St. Catharines, Ontario

Bound in Canada by: John Van Huizen Book Binding, St. Catharines, Ontario

The Haunted Press, (Division of 314340 Ontario Limited),

4219 Briarwood Avenue,

Niagara Falls, Ontario L2E 6Z1

Canadian Cataloguing in Publication Data

Foley, Robert J., 1941-

Niagara Story

Includes index

Contents: v. 1. Beginnings ---- v. 2. The War of 1812

ISBN 1-895528-00-3 (v. 1)   ISBN 1-895528-02-X (v. 2)

1. Niagara Peninsula (Ont.) - History. I. Title.

FC3095.N5F64 1994 971.338 C94-900997-0

F1059.N5F64 1994

Contents

Preface

This is the first volume of a series covering the feature that runs in the St. Catharines Standard as Niagara Story and in the Niagara Falls Review and Welland Tribune as Pioneer Days. This volume covers the initial twenty-five articles encompassing the time period, 12000 B.C. to 1812, from the retreat of the glacier through the coming of the first Homo Sapiens, the Neutral Indians, to the first European settlements. We will meet the first heroes that worked the land that we now call home.

This series of articles came out of a concern for the lack of knowledge and appreciation of the rich, exciting history that greets us at every turn in the Niagara Peninsula. The preception that Canadians have no identity as a people also spurred on the project.

Having lived in the United States for eight years I can assure you that we are distinct, we are different from our American cousins. Well then, where do we find that elusive Identity?

We start with where we have been as a people and a nation. We will find ourselves in the everyday joys and sorrows of our ancestors, in the lives of those who worked and loved and fought and died in this Niagara of ours.

This book is not meant to be a comprehensive history of the Niagara Peninsula, but rather, an attempt to bring to life our history through snapshots of the events that shaped the community that we live in today. To achieve this end I have included fictional narratives using dialogue and actions, which can not be documented. Although these narratives have no basis in fact, the persons were there and their words and actions are not out of the realm of possibility. To distinguish them from documented history they will appear in italics so that the reader may easily tell the two apart.

We must kindle a new interest in our history if we are to survive as a nation. If this series has advanced that aim in some small way then it can be judged a success.

Bob Foley

Niagara Falls, Ontario

December 31, 1993

ACKNOWLEDGEMENTS

A series such as this would not be possible without the commitment and courage of the editors of the various publications of the Niagara Peninsula. It all started in 1989 with Tim Dundas, then editor of the Regional Shopping News in Welland. Without hesitation he bought the concept of a weekly history series called Pioneer Days. His enthusiasm continued with his move to the Niagara Shopping News in Niagara Falls where Pioneer Days ran in both papers until the ravages of the recession took their toll. After a short break Lea Williams of the Niagara Falls Review and Jim Middleton of the Welland Tribune took up the vision and are now running Pioneer Days as a weekly feature. Murray Thompson and Kevin Cavanaugh of the St. Catharines Standard, in hard times, saw the importance of promoting local history and Niagara Story was born. I salute these men and women for their commitment to bringing our history to life.

No writer of history works in a vacuum. We all benefit by the work of those that went before us. I would especially like to acknowledge the work of George and Olive Seibel who together published the works of A.H. Tiplin in "Our Romantic Niagara" from which much of the geological material for this series was taken. George's work on the 200th anniversary of the Portage Road was invaluable in researching the early years of Niagara. A special mention must be made of Esther Summers, Thorold's official historian, whose knowledge of our history is unsurpassed. Often the temptation to take a shortcut in my research was brought up short by the question, "What will Esther say if I don't get it right?"

I would like to acknowledge the fine work of George Balbar in illustrating the series since January of 1991. His attention to detail and accuracy has added greatly to any success that the series has had in achieving its purpose.

Finally to the faithful readers of Pioneer Days and Niagara Story for their encouragement through phone calls and letters. It is the fuel that allows us to continue our journey through the Halls of History.

CHAPTER ONE

THE JOURNEY BEGINS

We will begin our journey in the last Ice Age when, what was to become, the Niagara Peninsula lay crushed under a mountain of snow and ice. This glacier may have been as much as two miles thick in some places. The glacier, although made up of ice and snow, had a elastic quality that allowed it to flow ever so slowly southward from the snow fields of Labrador. Its underside was a conglomeration of rocks, sand and clay that was dragged along as it marched relentlessly through the country side. This debris filled the ancient gorge that we call the St. David-Whirlpool Buried Gorge. This gorge ran in a line northwest from the whirlpool of the Niagara River, turning north through present day St. Davids. It passed west of Virgil on its way to Lake Ontario. A branch of this gorge cut northeast intersecting the Niagara River just north of McFarland House.

The glacier retreated from the Niagara area about twelve thousand years ago. The St. Lawrence Valley was still plugged with ice however and a large lake was formed. The beaches of this lake, called Lake Iroquois, were located at Queenston. The water was just eleven metres (35 ft.) below the average level of Queenston Heights.

The falls was born as waters swollen by the melting glacial ice sought an exit to Lake Iroquois. It found its outlet at Eldridge Terrace above Lewiston, New York. Like all new born babies this was a tiny falls in the beginning. The falls tumbling over the Niagara Escarpment was only eleven metres (35 ft.) high.

As the glacier retreated north the valley of the St. Lawrence became free of ice and Lake Iroquois began to recede. Eventually it became the lake we know as Ontario.

For the next four thousand years the falls slowly eroded the soft sandstone as it worked its way back to the Niagara Glen. Here a thin wedge of limestone split the falls in two for the first time. Unlike today, the major flow was on the east or American side of the river. The falls had grown up in those intervening years and now had a drop of two hundred and fifty feet.

The eastern falls eroded at a much faster rate and it soon cut behind the smaller western falls leaving a mass of rubble as the limestone island collapsed. This debris, along with boulders, loosed by the turbulent river, fell into the gorge creating the foundation for soil to accumulate and form the Niagara Glen.

It is likely that human eyes first saw the falls at this time. There is archeological evidence of human settlement in the London area about eleven thousand years ago. These people were the forbearers of the Neutral Indians who eventually settled here. Indians from several tribes came to hunt and fish in the pristine forests and streams as evidenced by the remains found in the peninsula.

It took the falls another seven thousand years to work its way back to the approximate location it is today. About a thousand years ago the falls split into two parts once again with the major flow going to the west side this time. With this split the roaring cataract set the stage for the human dramas that were to begin unfolding some three hundred years later.

The first human settlers of the Peninsula migrated here from the vicinity of London between 1300 and 1400 A.D. This Iroquoian group of Indians were called Atiouandaronk (they who understood the language) by the Hurons and the Attiragenrega by the Huron's perennial enemies, the Iroquois. The French eventually gave them the name Neutrals because of their unique position between the two warring nations.

The importance of this tribe in the political and cultural life of the area can be seen in its place in Iroquoian mythology. According to tradition, the Neutrals were the parent body of the ten tribes of the Iroquoian cultural group that included not just the five Nations: the Seneca, Mohawk, Oneida, Onondaga and Cayuga, but the Huron, Petun, Erie and Susquehannock as well. Among the Neutrals lived Jikonsaseh, "the mother of nations" or

"peace queen," who ruled over the league and non-league Iroquois alike. The people believed that she was a descendant of the first woman born on earth and she was always succeeded by her eldest daughter. She preserved the neutrality of the Neutral Nation as well as maintaining the military and political balance between Huron and Iroquois. Her village, called Keinuka, just east of the Niagara River, had a special status. It was North America's first peace court, the aboriginal equivalent to the World Court at the Hague.

Although it is difficult to assess the aboriginal population in the early days, it is estimated that, before the spread of European diseases among the tribes in the 1630s, there were between twenty and forty thousand Neutrals distributed in forty villages concentrated east of the Grand River in the Hamilton/Niagara district at the western end of Lake Ontario.

The Niagara Peninsula was rich in fish and game such as beaver, bear and deer. The soil was fertile and the Neutrals, unlike some of the other tribes, rarely went hungry in the winter months.

The Neutrals brought industry to the Niagara Peninsula long before the coming of the first Europeans. They were farmers, businessmen and traders and, perhaps, would not have been out of place in our own world of trade and commerce.

CHAPTER TWO
CIVILIZATION IN THE WILDERNESS

We often think of Canada's aboriginal peoples in the Hollywood image of whooping warriors living in tepees. When they were not hunting game for food they were making war on some neighbouring tribe. This image of the simple savage grunting his way through life has been handed down to us for generations.

In the Niagara Peninsula nothing could be farther from the truth. Over one hundred and fifty years before Europeans even knew that North America existed, an advanced political and economic system that rivaled that of the so called civilized world had developed here.

The Iroquois Confederacy, made up of the five nations: Mohawk, Seneca, Cayuga, Onondaga and Oneida, was a complicated alliance of nations that held together for four hundred years until the time of the American Revolution. This political system consisted of a series of checks and balances. Although the men ruled as chiefs and sat on the council, it was the women who controlled the economic resources of the tribe. Distribution of food was at the discretion of the matrons, the older women of the tribe. They could withhold food from the council or even war parties thus affecting the decisions made by these bodies. The matrons nominated the council elders, the highest assembly in the confederacy, and their advice was sought in matters of war and alliances with tribes outside the league. The women were designated as keepers of the longhouse thus dominating the domestic scene. They allocated tasks to be done by both the women and the men.

We have no precise record of the Neutral society, but they were Iroquoian and would have had a system based on the Iroquois model. They lived in palisaded villages with several families occupying a longhouse, several of which stood in a row within the walls.

The Neutrals were at peace with both the Hurons and the Iroquois. There is strong evidence that Neutral villages were considered sanctuary. If a warrior, hotly pursued by the enemy, could make it to a Neutral village he was safe from capture until he chose to venture out into the fields. The bitterest of enemies could meet in a Neutral village, but neither could make a hostile move against the other while there.

This neutral island in a sea of hostility has puzzled historians for years. Archeology has given rise to several interesting hypothesis as to the reason for this. One such theory involves the vast chert beds (a material essential to the manufacture of flint arrowheads) along the Niagara Escarpment. The Neutrals controlled this supply of material that was needed, not only for war, but for hunting as well. Both the Iroquois and Hurons were much too shrewd to make enemies of the tribe that controlled this resource. This theory was popular at the turn of the century and although it has given way to other theories, it still has some merit.

The second hypothesis is the "port of trade" theory. We will cover this idea in detail in a future article. Suffice to say that the peninsula appeared to be the centre of a complicated trading system that covered the greater part of North America.

The Neutrals were not, as their name might imply, a tribe of docile traders and farmers. They were described by early French explorers as fierce warriors, tall in stature. They constantly made war on the Atsisaehronons (Fire Nation) that occupied the land around Lake Michigan. This may have been trade related for many artifacts of western origin have been found in the various archeological digs in the peninsula. Perhaps the Neutrals were trespassing on the Fire Nation's turf.

The Niagara Peninsula was a major crossroads for travelers moving about the Great Lakes region. Many of the highways and roads we travel today were once part of a vast Indian trail system. Highway #8 that runs through St. Catharines to Hamilton was called the Mohawk Trail by the Indians. The Iroquois Trail ran from the location of Queenston along the plain between the escarpment and the lake, then swung west along present day

Highway #2 through Brantford and Wood-stock all the way to the Detroit River.

The trails were not only named, but they were also posted. The aboriginal traveler had signs to follow as clear as any highway markers we have today. You will notice, in George Balbar's illustration that accompanies this article, a tree that appears to be growing in a peculiar fashion. What you are seeing is the equivalent of a highway sign on the Indian trail system. Each trail had a unique tree design to identify it. A young sapling was tied in such a way that it would grow into a predetermined shape. A traveler knew what trail he was on by the shape of the tree markers.

The trail signs were renewed every so often to replace old and damaged trees. The tree shown in the illustration stood at the Sugar Loaf near Port Colborne and was still alive and healthy in the late 1960s. Another prime example of this method of marking trails may be seen on Highway #15 into Arnprior in the Ottawa Valley. Here the tree had two branches low on the main trunk tied down to form what looks like a candelabra. This tree, although still standing in 1990, appeared to be in bad shape.

4

CHAPTER THREE
WAR, TRADE AND COMMERCE

The social and political structure of the Iroquoian tribes, of which the Neutrals were one, was a delicate web of clan loyalties and interdependence. The family unit was too weak to face the rigors of survival on its own. Therefore the larger unit, the clan, bound together several families who shared the labour and the resources to their mutual benefit. The clan shared a longhouse in a village that consisted of a number of clans whose names were usually taken from the animal kingdom. Among the Seneca, for example, the eight clans were Wolf, Bear, Beaver, Turtle, Hawk, Snipe, Deer, and Heron.

The social rules of the day insisted that one always married outside his or her clan avoiding the problems created from the marriage of close relatives. Clan lineage was taken from the female side, thus, the man always went to live in the longhouse of his bride.

We have already seen that the economy of the Neutrals was dominated by the matrons or older women. They assigned the work for the clan and subsequently the village. Contrary to popular myths of the women doing all the heavy work, men were given the most strenuous jobs to do. When a new field was required it was the men who chopped down the trees and cleared the land. The women did the planting, tending of the crops and the grinding down of the grain into flour. Food preparation and preservation was also the job of the women. Hunting and fishing were an important source of food for the community and the men were responsible for this activity. Much of the men's energy was spent laying in meat and fish for the winter as well as for trade.

War was also an intricate part of the lives of the aboriginal peoples and men did the fighting. The village had to be constantly on the alert against raids from their traditional enemies. As we have already seen, the Neutrals, despite their relationship with the Iroquois and the Hurons, had enemies of their own.

The idea of neutral zones or buffers between warring tribes was not unique to the Eastern Woodlands Indians. There is evidence of such a zone between the Territories of the Chippewa and Sioux nations in Wisconsin and Minnesota. These zones lessened hostilities and allowed the sharing of game to the advantage of both tribes.

The Iroquois seemed to have refined this system of neutral zones. The confederacy was not only a loose alliance of the five nations, but included several tributary tribes. For example, the Cayugas defeated the Delawares in a war in 1712 and the Delawares were then adopted by the confederacy to serve as a buffer between the Iroquois and the Cherokees. The Delaware were forbidden to go to war unless called upon to do so by the Iroquois.

What is unique about the Neutral situation was their obvious independence and the length of time that it prevailed. The answer to the puzzle may lie in the "Port of Trade" hypothesis.

An extensive trade network embraced much of North America before the arrival of Europeans on this continent. Joseph Lafitau, considered the founder of scientific anthropology and a keen observer of the Indian way of life, wrote in 1724: " The savage nations have always traded with each other. Their trade is similar to that of antiquity, since it is a straight exchange of staples against staples. They all have something which the others do not have and the trade moves all these items from one group to the other. These consist of grain, wampum, furs, fur robes, tobacco, fish nets, canoes, clothes of moose hide, quills, meat from the hunt, cotton mats, cooking implements, calumet pipes, in short everything that is used for sustaining human life."

In order to facilitate this trade in an uncertain military climate where hostile tribes might come into contact with one another, a place where safety was guaranteed was required. The Neutrals appeared to supply this place.

The function of this "Port of Trade" was to provide military security to the Neutrals, civil

protection to the traders, facilities for storage of goods and agreement on the relative value of those goods. The Neutrals were the middlemen of the complex trading network that functioned for two hundred years.

The Neutrals occupied territory that was on the border of two ecological zones. To the north the Hurons occupied the agricultural region of the southeast shore of Georgian Bay. The Hurons carried on trade with the more northerly hunting and gathering Algonkian tribes exchanging corn, nets and tobacco for skins, dried fish, birch bark canoes and meat. These commodities in turn were traded, to the Neutrals for tobacco, black squirrel skins and the famous "Erie Stones". These stones had value in curing wounds. Le Sieur Francois Gendron visited the Neutrals in 1643 and he wrote: "At the bottom of certain rocks a foam was forming from the bounding waters and becoming a stone or rather a petrified salt which has a slight yellow tinge, which possessed the fine virtue of curing some purulent (infected) wounds and malignant ulcers."

The Neutrals also played an important role in the movement of luxury goods from far to the south. A type of oyster shell used in making wampum belts and stombus, a large conch shell, from the Gulf of Mexico were a regular trade item in the Peninsula. Shells from the southeast coast of the United States passed from the Susquehannocks through the Neutrals to the northern tribes.

The Neutrals also were big traders of Raccoon skin robes from the Eries as well as gourds from further south used for storing oil. The Neutrals did not passively sit here and receive goods. Their status with the Iroquois and Hurons allowed them to move freely through their respective territories. The old adage, "you get the best deal at the source of supply," was not lost on the first inhabitants of the Niagara Peninsula.

The first Europeans reached the Peninsula in 1615. This incursion spelled the beginning of the end for the Neutral Indians.

CHAPTER FOUR
THE DISPERSAL OF THE NEUTRALS

The first European to visit the Neutrals is thought to have been Etienne Brule who reached the peninsula in 1615. His description of the country prompted Joseph de la Roche Daillon, a French Recollect priest, to winter among the Neutrals in 1626.

The delicate position of the Neutrals vis-a-vis the other tribes in the area can be shown by the efforts of the Hurons to discourage contact between the French and the Neutrals. Daillon met hostility when he went to the Neutrals because of Huron propaganda. He wrote: "In a word, the Hurons told them so much evil of us to prevent their going to trade; That the French were unapproachable, rude, sad, melancholy people, who lived only on snakes and poison; that we eat thunder...that we all had a tail like animals; that the women...bear five or six children at one time, adding a thousand other absurdities to make us hated by them and prevent their trading with us." However, the Hurons as well as the Ottawa did not object to the French trading with the Neutrals but, to their wintering among them with the inference of a more permanent relationship.

The two Jesuits, Brebeuf and Lalemont, who were to be killed by the Iroquois in 1649, met the same hostility in 1640. The Neutrals knew how delicate the political situation was. Peace gifts were refused by them. They declared: "Do you not know...the danger in which you put the country?"

It seems obvious that by the 1640s relations between the Iroquois and the Neutrals were strained. It has been suggested that the growing trade with the Dutch and the English made the Neutrals less important in the scheme of things. The introduction of firearms reduced the Iroquois dependency on flint for arrowheads and subsequently their need for the Neutral services.

The survival of the Neutrals clearly rested upon the maintenance of the military/political balance between the Iroquois and the Hurons. Apparently the shift in the political situation began as early as 1630 when mounting tensions between the Neutrals and the Hurons led the latter to prepare for war. The crisis passed however and war was averted.

The fateful year for the first inhabitants of the peninsula was 1649. In that year several large war parties of the Iroquois Confederancy gathered in upstate New York for the largest raid ever launched on Huron territory. The Hurons, decimated by European diseases that they had no way of fighting off, were no match for the onslaught that descended on their villages.

On the morning of March 16, 1649 the French at Ste Marie among the Hurons looked on with dismay as a rising pillar of smoke curled into the sky in the distance. What did it mean? Their answer was not long in coming. A straggling line of refugees from the village of St. Louis with three survivors from St. Ignace collapsed at the gates. With furtive glances over their shoulders the three told of the attack of the Iroquois and the swift fall of the village.

Meanwhile at St. Louis, eight Huron warriors prepared to fight a thousand Mohawk and Seneca braves. The Huron chief, Stephen Annaotaha, urged the two Jesuits, Brebeuf and Lalemont, to flee to Ste. Marie, but the two decided to stay and share the fate of their tiny flock. The village was soon overwhelmed and the Hurons quickly killed or captured. The two missionaries were tortured to death.

The Hurons were scattered to the winds. Refugees poured into Neutral villages for sanctuary relying on the age old custom for protection. Tradition dictated that once inside the palisades all were safe. However, when the victorious Mohawk and Seneca warriors arrived before the gates they demanded that the refugees be turned over to them.

At first the Neutrals refused citing the law of sanctuary. However, the Iroquois would not be denied and they threatened to attack the villages to obtain their prisoners. The hapless Hurons were sent to their fate.

Many underwent torture as was the custom among the Indians at that time.

Others were adopted into the tribe, another custom among the Iroquois. Even warriors were adopted taking the tribe as their own.

Suddenly the whole reason for the Neutrals existence was destroyed. No longer need the Iroquois fear a powerful enemy to the north. Trade had shifted east where Albany, New York was the new neutral zone. The fate of the Neutrals was sealed.

The old shaman made the long trek to the Falls of Onguiaaha to listen to the voices of the Thunder Spirits that lived behind the great cataract. He sat upon a flat rock that protruded over the river and prayed to the thunder god, Hinum. "What is to become of my people?"

The wind, which had been blowing steadily from the west, slowly shifted around to the east drenching the old man with spray. Sadly the old shaman rose and walked away. The thunder god was weeping for his people.

In 1652 the Senecas, the Neutral's closest neighbour of the Iroquois Confederacy, attacked, utterly destroying or killing anything or anyone they could not carry off. The Neutrals ceased to exist as a nation and those who escaped or were captured were absorbed into either the Iroquois or some other tribe to the north or west.

The land of the Neutrals came under the control of the Mississaugas but strangely they did not attempt to settle this fertile land. The ghosts of the Neutrals ruled over the forests and meadows of the Niagara Peninsula for 130 years until the loyalists such as Isaac Dolson and the Secords cast longing eyes at the pristine forested lands of Niagara.

CHAPTER FIVE
THE COMING OF THE WHITE MAN

With the dispersal of the Neutral Indians in 1652 the Peninsula lay in peace for over a hundred years except for the occasional passage of Indian parties along the many trails that crisscrossed it. However, the east bank of the river was a veritable beehive of activity.

Rene-Robert Cavalier, Sieur de La Salle visited the east bank in 1669 and returned in 1679 to establish the portage that was to bypass the great falls to facilitate the movement of the goods of the fur trade. It ran from just above the falls at Fort Schlosser opposite Chippawa along the modern Portage Avenue in Niagara Falls, New York to present day Lewiston, New York.

It was over this portage that LaSalle's men manhandled the tools and equipment to build the first ship to ply the upper lakes, the Griffin. The keel was laid at the mouth of Cayuga Creek just above the falls on January 22, 1679. The ship was launched and set sail that spring, but was lost on the return trip to Niagara.

To protect the portage LaSalle built the first fort to occupy the site of Fort Niagara. LaSalle called it Fort Conde. This first attempt ended when the fort was accidentally burned to the ground.

In 1687 the French made another attempt to protect the fur trade route. The Governor of New France, Jacques-Rene de Brisay, Marquis de Denonville, organized a major operation against the Senecas which only succeeded in burning a few villages and killing some hogs. An old Huron chief had warned Denonville that if he stirred the wasps' nest he had better swat the wasps. The expedition failed to do that and the French paid the price for many years afterward.

On abandoning the campaign Denonville had a fort built on the same site as Fort Conde that they called Fort Denonville. This was another ill starred venture. The garrison lacked provisions and the Seneca Indians, fully aroused after Denonville's handiwork, prevented the soldiers from foraging for food. In the spring of 1688 the relieving party found only twelve of the one hundred man garrison still alive. The fort was regarrisoned but soon afterward the French took inventory, pulled down the stockade and abandoned the site. Through all this the west bank of the river was left to the ghosts of the Neutrals.

For the next thirty-eight years no attempt was made to reestablish a post here. However, in 1726 the French renewed their friendship with the Seneca through the influence of Chabert Joncaire who had married a Seneca woman. They asked permission to establish a trading post at Niagara. They got their permission, but were not allowed to build a fort. The French used a little deception at this point and built a large stone building that they called the "House of Peace." It was in fact a castle that could be easily defended. The building is still part of Old Fort Niagara today. This stone castle was named "La Maison a Machicoulis de Niagara". Even the French garrison troops of the time found this to be a mouthful and they began to refer to their post as "Fort de Niagara".

To help insure the continued cooperation of the Seneca Joncaire became the portage master. Under his direction the French employed about two hundred Indians to help carry the goods up the escarpment at the Landing (Lewiston). The road up the escarpment at the Landing was so steep that the Seneca called it "Duh-jih-heh-oh or "The Crawl on all Fours".

Over the ensuing years additions were made to the post at the mouth of the river, but a major expansion did not occur until 1755 when the fort reached the proportions that we see today. By this time the "House of Peace" was a fort in every sense of the word.

In that same year a traveler, who crossed the portage, wrote: "On this carrying place I saw about two hundred Indians, most of them belonging to the Six Nations, busy carrying packs of furs, chiefly of deer and beavers, over the Carry-Place. It is surprising to see what quantities of goods are brought every day to this carrying place. An Indian has twenty pence for every pack he carries and

he dearly earns it for the distance is near three leagues."

The British besieged the fort in 1759 and the French surrendered after nineteen days. The British took effective control of the portage from that time. They made some early mistakes with the Senecas that was to lead to a tragedy a few years later.

One of the first moves the British made was to grade the road up the escarpment at the Landing so that goods could be carried exclusively by wagon. This put the Seneca porters out of work. In 1763 the Ottawa chief, Pontiac, led a revolt and the disgruntled Senecas joined in.

On the morning of September 14, 1763 a wagon train of twelve carts moved along the portage led by the wagon master John Stedman. At the point above the cave known as the Devil's Hole five hundred Seneca warriors lay in ambush in the dense forest that bordered the road.

The warriors struck and with the attackers on one side and the gorge on the other, the outnumbered soldiers were soon killed. John

Stedman was captured, but as the warriors led his horse away he managed to cut the reins and make his escape.

The garrison at the lower landing heard the shots and rushed to the rescue. They ran into a second ambush and all but eight of them perished. Eighty British soldiers were killed and the wagons and draft animals were thrown into the gorge.

Meanwhile, the Niagara Peninsula remained in quiet slumber. The one exception was the old French trading post at Fort Erie. In 1764 the British under General Bradstreet's chief engineer, Captain Montresor, built a fort where Lake Erie enters the Niagara. Appropriately, the post was called Fort Erie.

The fate of the Peninsula was not decided at Fort Niagara or at the seat of power in far off London, but near Boston, Massachusetts on April 19, 1775. British troops, attempting to disarm the Massachusetts Militia, were fired upon and defeated at the battles of Concord and Lexington. The American Revolution was on and although no one knew it at the time, the Peninsula's future was settled.

CHAPTER SIX
NIAGARA: A LOYALIST REFUGE

With the threat of the French in Quebec removed the American colonists began to resent the taxation of the British government to pay for the defense of the colonies during the long French and Indian Wars. It had long been the practice to raise at least part of the cost of defending the empire by taxing goods shipped into the ports of the Atlantic seaboard. In 1774 the famous Boston Tea Party took place. Several men disguised as Indians dumped a load of tea into the harbour at Boston to protest a tax levied on that commodity. Soon afterward shots were fired and the revolution was on.

At the beginning of the American Revolution the colonists could be broken down into three groups: one third were rebels, one third loyalists and one third just wanted to be left alone to raise their families and get on with the business of survival. The rebels flocked to join the Continental Army or formed local militia units. The loyalists joined the British Army or formed rival militias, while the rest attempted to go about their affairs taking no sides. Those who tried to sit on the fence eventually had to choose and those that supported the crown, along with the original loyalists, were among those who settled in the Peninsula. Once fighting started in earnest almost everyone was forced to pick a side. Sometimes the decision depended on who got to them first. When faced with the choice of joining the Continental Army or being hanged as a loyalist, an instant rebel was often born.

Who were these loyalists? Who were these people who would have such a profound effect on our future? Those that would become known as United Empire Loyalists conjure up a picture of stout English stock fighting for king and country. Although this was true in many cases there were others among the loyalists who were immigrants to the American colonies from all over Europe. Many that eventually settled here came from the Palatine region of Germany and were known as the Pennsylvania Dutch. The name Dutch comes from a corruption of the word "Deutsch" that these German immigrants used to describe themselves. Many of the people who fought for the British were native born Americans of varying ethnic backgrounds.

One of these loyalists was John Butler whose family had settled in the Mohawk Valley of New York. He was forced to flee his home and in 1777 formed a corps of rangers to fight for the British cause. They eventually became known as Butler's Rangers. Along with his son Walter he led raids into New York and Pennsylvania in conjunction with their Indian allies to deprive the rebels of food and to tie down the Continental Army.

The first settlers in Niagara Falls were the family of Philip Bender who was born in Germany and emigrated to New Jersey after 1750 with his Dutch wife. They fled to Fort Niagara for refuge in 1776 and Philip joined the Rangers in 1778. There are a number of examples of non English loyalists who gave up everything to fight for the king.

The Secords, James and Peter, joined Butler's Rangers in March of 1777 and were among the first settlers to cross the river and settle at Queenston. Haggai Skinner attempted to join the loyal forces in 1778 but was captured and spent the entire war in custody. He eventually settled in Stamford Township.

What made these settlers reject American republicanism? Often it was not so much a love of the king as a fear of the anarchy that was born out of the mobs who tarred and feathered known loyalists or worse, hanged them on the spot. Many had fled religious and political persecution in Europe and were not prepared to face the same again.

The raids into New York and Pennsylvania were personal crusades for some of these men who had been robbed of their worldly possessions and sometimes were run out of town on a sharp rail or tarred and feathered.

Revenge was a spur that drove the Rangers to great achievements in the raids they undertook. They fought amid hardships and hunger that they would have not tolerated in normal circumstances.

The Revolution proved to be the downfall of the Iroquois Confederacy. The Indians could not understand how their English friends could be fighting among themselves. The initial stance of the confederacy was to remain neutral. However, it became apparent early in the conflict that this would prove difficult if not impossible. The strain of divided loyalties was too much for the alliance to bear.

As early as 1710 a number of Iroquois chiefs had visited England and pledged their support for the English king. Among them was John Brant grandfather of Joseph Brant who was to be such a prominent figure in the raids originating from Fort Niagara. Who were the proper heirs to this pledge, American or British?

Joseph Brant was born in the Ohio region about 1742 and was educated at the Anglican Mohawk mission. After a visit to England in 1776 Brant was convinced that the Six nations' fortune rested with the British cause. Brant also feared the territorial expansionist attitude of the American colonists. He urged the confederacy to side with the British. The Oneida and the Tuscarora leaned in the direction of the Americans and the others wanted to side with the British or remain neutral. A number of attempts were made to call a council, but the Seneca refused to attend. The warriors were seriously divided and the confederacy split. The council fire went out at the Six Nations capital at Onondaga and the power of the Iroquois was broken.

With the intervention of the French in 1778 the fortunes of war swung to the Americans and it soon became evident that the Rangers and their families would not be returning to their homes to the south. Anxious eyes were cast in the direction of the slumbering forests of Niagara.

CHAPTER SEVEN

SETTLEMENT COMES TO NIAGARA

The ever present pressure of feeding the garrison of Fort Niagara and the swelling band of refugees that daily staggered into the area eventually forced the authorities to consider alternate means of supplying the needs of a crowded post far from the main base of supply. One scheme was for the refugees to produce food on crown land until the end of the war.

A letter to one Captain Robison from Fort Niagara dated 4 August 1779 stated: "Dolson is very anxious to leave the house as he and the Secords are going to farm it on the opposite side of the river facing the Landing." The government resisted the move out of concern for the Royal Proclamation in 1763 which gave the Indians all the land west of the Niagara.

Peter Secord, along with his brother James, stood at the Landing and gazed with a mixture of excitement and misgivings at the far shore. Colonel John Butler had given them permission, with three others, the Dolsons, Showers and Lutes, to establish farms on the west bank. So, with what little they had managed to salvage from their former homes in the rebellious colonies to the south and what they had been able to scrounge from the government, they were about to cross into a virtual wilderness. They hoped to feed their families and have some food left over to sell to the military garrison at Fort Niagara.

The boat shoved off and, using the back eddies in close to shore, made its way up river before striking out into the mainstream and allowing the current to carry them down to the bank opposite the landing. They scrambled ashore and were greeted by stands of virgin forest of Black Walnut, Hickory, Oak and Maple among others. The huge trees with their accompanying underbrush made the hearts of these stout men sink. A formidable task lay ahead. What if the rains failed to come? What if the Indians objected, forcing the government to move them back to the east bank?

Even if all went well the group had no guarantee that they could remain on the land.

It was strictly understood that it was crown land they were settling on and that the arrangements were only temporary to feed their families and the garrison. It was thought that after the war all would return to their former homes south of the border to reclaim their land.

James Secord awoke before dawn and prepared for the coming day. There was a "bee" scheduled to build a shanty for his family. When all were gathered and it was light enough to see they laid out the square for the house on a flat piece of ground and located the trees that had been marked earlier for the walls.

James acted as captain with Isaac Dolson as corner man and the work began. As each log was cut to length it was notched top and bottom so that it would fit into the cross piece below it. The corner man was responsible to see that the notches were properly cut and the captain supervised the placing of the logs. The fireplace was made from logs lined with clay and the chimney was built with split sticks lined in the same way as the fireplace. The planking for the floor was split and laid and finally the clapboard roof was put in place, secured by weight poles that reached across the roof. A piece of greased paper covered the tiny window next to the door allowing some light to come into the interior.

The clapboard door was finally hung using leather for hinges and the space between the logs was filled with mud and moss. The one room Secord mansion was ready for occupation.

While the men toiled at building the cabin the women were not idle. A huge kettle hung over an open fire where a meal was cooked for the noon break and for dinner later in the day. For lunch the hard working crew was treated to salt pork and a pot of soup. Mrs. Secord also baked a fish pie with potatoes. The meal included fresh baked bread, sliced dried pumpkin and black berries that the children had picked the day before. After a brief respite the men were back at it until the job was completed.

With the door hung and everything double checked the men sat down at the split log table for a well deserved dinner which consisted of more salt pork, a shoulder of venison and fried corn porridge with maple sugar. "Coffee" was made using dried corn and barley. After all had eaten their fill someone pulled out a fiddle and laughter and music rang through the twilight and on into the night.

The next major hurdle was the clearing of the land. It had to be cleared acre by back breaking acre. James, with his four children, began by cutting away the underbrush among the trees. This he gathered up into bundles to be burned. Next some of his neighbours came over and they began felling the huge trees that covered the acres that James intended to plant the following spring.

With the ring of the axe reverberating through the air, tree after tree came crashing to the ground. Once they were stripped they were rolled together into piles for burning.

This ritual was repeated over and over through that summer and fall until all was ready for the coming spring.

In May of 1781 Colonel John Butler negotiated the purchase of a four mile strip of land along the Niagara from the Mississauga Indians. The following year eleven additional families moved across and the census taken by Butler gives us an idea of the extent of the new community.

The census showed that our first group had been busy indeed. James Secord had cleared twenty acres; Isaac Dolson, thirty acres; Peter Secord, twenty-four acres and Michael Showers, twelve acres. The sixteen families consisted of sixty-eight people as well as forty-nine horses, forty-two cows, nineteen heifers and one hundred and three hogs. The crops grown in the peninsula at that time were Indian corn, wheat, oats, pumpkins and potatoes.

The peninsula was awake at last.

CHAPTER EIGHT
LIFE ON THE FRONTIER

By the fall of 1782 there were sixteen families established on the west bank of the Niagara. The original five had been joined by several other loyalists. Most were veterans of Butler's Rangers who were no longer fit for service either by reason of age or illness.

Initially the pioneers settled on one hundred acres each running north from Queenston Heights toward present day Niagara-on-the-Lake where Butler had established the headquarters of the Rangers some years earlier. They were very anxious about the status of their lands. Although John Butler was lobbying to get them title to the acreage under cultivation, the governor, General Frederick Haldimand, was reluctant to change the arrangement under which the loyalists had taken up the land. However, with the war going badly for the British, Haldimand decided to ask for instructions from England forwarding the petitions of John Butler with his own assessment of the situation. They could only wait for the letters to reach England and a reply to come back.

Madeline Secord surveyed her morning's work with some satisfaction. She had finished off six pounds of tallow in making candles. She employed the dip method using the big kitchen kettle, which she filled half full of hot water. Six cotton wicks were then attached to a stick about two feet long. Tallow was put into the kettle which melted and stayed on top of the water. When all was ready Madeline began dipping the wicks through the floating tallow allowing them to pick up a little each time they passed through. This process continued until the candles had reached their desired thickness. Now they hung suspended between two saplings to harden.

She eyed them critically for she had doubts as to their quality. She had only managed eight to the pound and the wick material was not as good as it should have been. She had produced as high as a dozen to the pound back home on the Susquehanna River in Pennsylvania. Some of those now hanging before her would sputter and smoke but it could not be helped.

It was October 1783 and their second crop was coming in. Her husband James was off with Isaac Dolson to bring in James' brother Peter's corn. Thursday they would get in Dolson's and then it would be their turn. Their son, James Jr., was busy stacking wood for the winter. He was too young to split it but he could slowly build up the ready use pile near the cabin door.

She turned to gaze at the one room cabin that they called home. She could see places in the log wall where more mud would have to be packed before the snow came. It was at times like these that she missed her old home on the Susquehanna the most. She brightened a little remembering that James had promised that they would build a new house next year of squared logs with a peaked roof to allow for a loft for storage and to double as a bedroom for the children. He even promised real glass for the windows instead of the greased paper that covered the one by the front door now. This winter James was also going to make her a proper chair and she had already begun to gather materials to upholster it.

The life of a pioneer woman left little time for dreaming and Madeline was off to grind some wheat into flour to supply the family with bread that winter and supplement the rations from the government at Fort Niagara. As yet there was no grist mill within reach and the tedious task had to be done by hand.

She took the basket of thrashed grain to the stump that they had labourously hollowed out in the spring. They had burned and scraped until they had made a deep, smooth cavity. After pouring some of the grain into the hollow she took the pestle, a large sapling with the root end rounded to facilitate the grinding process, and began pounding the grain by raising the pole above her head and bringing it down sharply to pulverize it. Fortunately the children loved to help with this task and she was assured of a break or two that afternoon.

Later, with the children grinding grain, Madeline turned her attention to the crude

oven located in the yard for baking bread. She got a good fire going and went to see if the dough had risen. This brought a frown to her brow as the quality of the yeast was very suspect. She breathed a sigh of relief as she raised the blanket covering the dough.

The children had tired of grinding and had run off to gather kindling and pick berries for dinner. Before getting back to the wheat Madeline cleared the smoldering embers from her oven, swept the bottom clean and carefully placed the bread into it to bake using the long handled wooden pallet that had been carved from a single piece of pine.

About four o'clock Madeline went in to see how their dinner was coming. This was a special night as James had gone out before leaving for the harvest and shot a plump tom turkey and one of the children was patiently turning the spit in the fireplace watching with fascination as the skin turned a golden brown and the juice, dripping on to the glowing embers, hissed in protest.

When James Secord arrived home the family sat down to a rare feast indeed. After saying the blessing they merrily ate roast turkey, pumpkin and corn with fresh baked bread to sop up the drippings and blackberries to top off the meal. A feast fit for King George himself.

After supper Madeline sat by the light of a candle and mended James' shirt that had been damaged in the day's work. When all the little chores were completed, including feeding the live stock and securing them for the night James and Madeline gratefully turned in themselves in anticipation of another long day that would begin before the sun was up.

HISTORICAL NOTE: The land occupied by these early settlers was located to the north of present day Highway #8A at the bottom of the escarpment at Queenston. Isaac Dolson held one hundred acres that ran from the river bank back to the First Concession Road. James Secord's land would have been the next hundred acres running from the First Concession to the Second Concession. From Queenston Heights you can gaze down upon the land first settled by our pioneer ancestors.

CHAPTER NINE

THE LOYALISTS: NEW BEGINNINGS

Notice of the signing of the Treaty of Paris, which ended the War of the American Revolution reached Niagara on April 26, 1783. Shortly after this Brigadier General Allan MacLean wrote to General Haldimand: "Colonel Butler says that none of his people will ever think of going to attend Courts of Law in the Colonies, where they could not expect a shadow of justice, and that to repurchase their estates is what they are not able to do . . . and they would rather go to Japan then go among the Americans, where they could never live in peace."

With the end of hostilities the settlers became most anxious to clarify their status regarding the land they had settled. All hope of a return to their former homes ended with the American victory. John Butler continually pressed Haldimand for a favourable answer, but he would not budge until instructions came from Britain.

MacLean wrote Haldimand in May of 1783 attaching petitions from Isaac Dolson, Elijah Phelps, Thomas McMicking and Donald Bee. They asked for leases to their land that would offer them some security from eviction. At the same time they promised to sell their excess produce to the garrison commander at Niagara for a reasonable price. Haldimand was still awaiting instructions but assured the settlers that he would give them every consideration.

The king signed the royal proclamation laying down the policy for land grants to the loyalists on July 1, 1783. However, the notice did not reach Quebec by the end of the navigation season on the St. Lawrence and the pioneers had to wait in suspense for the news. In anticipation of a favourable reply Colonel Butler began negotiating the purchase of land from the Mississauga Indians during the winter of 1783-84.

The royal proclamation finally reached Haldimand in the spring of 1784. He immediately ordered Butler to complete the purchase of the land between Lakes Erie and Ontario for distribution to the loyalists.

The grants were given as follows: to every head of a household, one hundred acres; to each member of his family, fifty acres; to single men, fifty acres; to every non-commissioned officer, two hundred acres plus fifty acres for each member of his family; every private, one hundred acres with his family provided fifty acres each. The land was to be divided and lots drawn by those wishing to settle. Those already on the land were allowed to keep the property that they had cleared for cultivation. Once the lots were drawn and located there was some trading of land to be near family or old neighbours.

In addition each family was to be provided with the necessary tools to get them started. The implements to be supplied were: one felling axe for each male over the age of fourteen, one ploughshare and coulter, leather for horse collars, two spades, three iron wedges, fifteen iron harrow teeth (used to break up clods in the soil), three hoes, one inch and one half inch auger, three assorted chisels, one gouge (a type of chisel), three gimblets (a small drill like tool), one hand saw, assorted files, one nail hammer, one drawing knife, one frow for splitting shingles, two scythes, one sickle, and a broad axe. For every three families a grind stone was issued. The animals allotted to each family were: two horses, two cows and six sheep. Seed for their initial crop included: wheat, Indian corn, peas, oats, potatoes and flax. The settlers also requested that a blacksmith be established in each settlement with tools and support for two years. Clothing was also allotted to the families to get them started.

The purchase of the Indian land was completed on May 22, 1784. Butler's Rangers were disbanded on the 24th of June and Butler made preparations for distribution of lots. Near the end of July he sent a report listing the rangers and other loyalists who wished to take up residence on the west bank of the Niagara. The list included two hundred and fifty-six men, ninety-nine women, one hundred and fifteen children under ten years of age and one hundred and forty-eight over ten for a total of six hundred and twenty-nine people. Most of the rangers and their families

settled in the northern part of the peninsula between the Twelve Mile Creek and the Niagara.

It was July 1784. Christian Stoner crossed the Niagara from Black Rock to Fort Erie and began to explore the wilderness along the shores of Lake Erie. He sat astride his horse and viewed the surrounding country with a brief nod of approval. The authorities had told him that the hill on which he found himself was called the Sugar Loaf, one of the few features on an otherwise flat landscape. To the west was a great marsh and to the east another smaller parcel of swampy ground. Around the Sugar Loaf and further north the soil was as rich as he had ever seen. Yes, this would due nicely. This was the land flowing with milk and honey promised in the bible.

Christian Stoner was a Mennonite. He had ridden from his home in Lancaster County, Pennsylvania in search of a new home for his family and, perhaps, other Mennonite families who felt uncomfortable in the new republic of the United States.

During the revolution the Mennonites had refused to take sides because of the pacifism of their sect. Although they were not as harshly treated as the loyalists, they were heavily taxed and some harassment had taken place. Signs of an intolerant society were beginning to manifest themselves and the Mennonites had no desire to live under a cloud for the rest of their lives.

Christian Stoner turned his horse back toward Fort Erie determined to inquire about the availability of land in this wilderness. It is possible that Stoner may have visited Fort Niagara to test the reception any attempt to settle the area near Fort Erie might receive. The British authorities were anxious to populate the area as a bulwark against American expansion. The Mennonite from Pennsylvania would have been given assurances that those prepared to swear allegiance to the crown would be welcome. It was to be two years before Stoner's dream was to be realized.

CHAPTER TEN
OF GRIST MILLS AND MIGRATION

Daniel Servos, a captain in Butler's Rangers, stood near the mouth of the Four Mile Creek surveying the grist mill that was under construction. It was the summer of 1783 and, with government backing, he was building the first mills in the Niagara Peninsula to grind grain and cut lumber for the fledgling settlements. David Brass, a former sergeant in the rangers, who was overseeing the construction, assured him that both the grist and saw mills would be in full operation by the time the crops were harvested.

The dams were finished and the buildings well on their way to completion. It was only the thought of the parts promised by the government that caused him concern. The mill stones and gears for the grist mill as well as the blades and other equipment for the saw mill had to come by bateaux and schooner from Montreal. With the proliferation of settlements and the corresponding demand for supplies, it would not take much to throw the whole project off schedule. A shipwreck or overturned bateaux in the rapids of the St. Lawrence could lose a whole year for the Servos mills. The needs of the garrison at Fort Niagara gave the delivery of his materials priority. This was the only thing that eased his mind as they awaited word of the shipment's arrival.

Daniel Servos' grandfather, Christopher, came to America in 1726 after a long career in the army of one of the smaller German states. He settled on the Charlotte River near Schoharie, New York. The family prospered, operating mills and farming a large tract of land.

At the outbreak of the American Revolution the Servos family chose to remain loyal to the British Crown. In 1777, after being harassed and threatened, they were forced to flee their home. Daniel made his way to Fort Niagara where he enlisted in the rangers. He rose to the rank of captain and was probably discharged early in 1783. He immediately put plans in motion to set up mills in the Niagara Peninsula.

Servos named his complex at the Four

Mile Creek "Palatine Hill" after the Servos' ancestral home in the German Palatinate. In the years following he added a tannery, blacksmith shop, furniture making shop, potashery, cider mill and general store. People walked from Niagara as well as from the Twelve Mile Creek to shop at the well stocked store at Palatine Hill.

*****

It was October 1784. Isaac Dolson, with his family possessions loaded on a wagon pulled by a yoke of oxen, waited patiently for the large flat bottomed boat that served as a ferry to come over from the East Landing and take his family across. He was glad of the delay for it gave him and his family more time to bid farewell to their neighbours who had come to see them off.

They were particularly sorry to leave the Secords who had been their neighbours to the west. His wife was embracing Madeline secord and tears flowed as the two friends said goodbye, probably never to see each other again. James Secord's attempts to talk him out of the move had failed. Uncertainty over the title to the land and the fact that his son, Matthew, was prospering in Detroit as a merchant had made up his mind for him. He purchased a farm from Theophile LeMay for five hundred pounds at Petit Cote on the east bank of the Detroit River. His decision was made easier by his son-in-law who bought the adjoining property and was to follow in a week or two.

After much back slapping and tears the wagon rumbled onto the ferry. The Dolsons began a journey that took them over the eastern portage to Fort Schlosser where they boarded a schooner to take them to their new home. After lowering the oxen into the hold and securing the wagon on deck they sailed for Amherstburg on the Detroit River at the far end of Lake Erie.

At the same time that Isaac Dolson was moving his family, Christian Stoner was reporting to his Mennonite neighbours in Lancaster County, Pennsylvania, on what he

had discovered in Upper Canada. The discussions went far into the night and in the end Stoner told them that he intended to move his family as soon as the availability of land grants was established. Abraham Neff and Christian Knisley nodded their approval and agreed to accompany him.

In the summer of 1787 the three families sold their land and began the long trek to Canada. With their oxen pulling their worldly possessions they headed north up the Susquehanna Valley through Harrisburg and up through Williamsport. They took the forest trail that followed, roughly, Highway #15 today. The trail was narrow and rutted bogging down the wagons on a number of occasions. Even the patient oxen bellowed in protest and had to be coaxed along.

After entering New York State they turned northwest toward Buffalo. Their route took them through Bath, Danville, Geneseo, and Batavia.

The three men stood on the wharf at Black Rock, New York and stared across the fast flowing Niagara River at the far shore. It had been a long arduous journey, but, they had made it without incident. After a brief prayer of thanksgiving they prepared to load the first wagon on the ferry. When all was secured the ferrymen rowed up river using the back eddies to assist them before striking out into the current. They allowed it to sweep them down toward the landing on the west side.

As Christian Stoner stepped ashore he knew that he had made the right decision. After wintering near Fort Erie they planned to take up their land in a new country for a new beginning.

HISTORIAL NOTE: The date 1787 used as the year that the Mennonite families left Lancaster County has been arbitrarily picked by the author. Evidence indicates that this event took place sometime between 1786 and 1789.

CHAPTER ELEVEN

MENNONITES SETTLE HUMBERSTONE

It was cold and damp that November day in 1787 as Christian Stoner, Abraham Neff and Christian Knisley made their way back to their encampment near Fort Erie where they planned to winter with their families. They had been to the fort to settle their land grants and to pick up supplies for the long cold months ahead. The next morning they would set out to locate and stake out their homesteads in the wilderness south of the Chippawa Creek and to the north of the Sugar Loaf.

They decided to walk using the pack horse lent to them by the fort commander to carry equipment and food for the journey. From his earlier exploration of the area Stoner knew that the trails were narrow and they would make better time on foot. Trying to move a wagon through the bush at this season of the year would have been foolhardy. He looked up at the sky just as the bone chilling rain began to fall.

Dawn greeted the Mennonite families with a cold, misty drizzle that explored every opening in the layers of clothing they wore. The men bid farewell and headed into the bleak morning mist.

Their route took them west along the old Indian trail that hugged the Lake Erie shoreline. The rain had turned the pathway into a quagmire and the going was slow. They fought the mud that sucked at their shoes as if to draw them deep into the bowels of the earth itself.

The horse struggled for her footing, registering a protest now and again by tossing her head. Often the unlucky man leading her went sprawling in the muck along the trail.

After covering a mere 21 miles they decided to make camp near Point Albino at the junction of the north-south trail. They would be leaving the lake here and traveling north the next day.

After seeing to the horse the three men pitched their tent in the shelter of the forest and managed to cook their first decent meal of the day. They ate in silence, each coping with the depression brought on by a chill dampness that penetrated everything.

The next morning dawned cold and overcast, but the rain had stopped and there was a promise of clearing in the air. Everything lay in a blanket of frost as the three men cooked and ate their breakfast. Stoner was confident that they could reach their destination by noon.

As the morning wore on a sense of excitement came over these usually sober men. A new land and a new life free from the bias' of their American neighbours.

As Stoner had predicted, they reached his land grant by early afternoon in what was to become Humberstone Township. He surveyed his holdings with some satisfaction. Although there was the arduous task of clearing the land and building a house, he knew that the soil was rich and would provide his family with a comfortable living.

They began marking out trees for felling to clear acreage for planting and for building a house before moving on to locate the lands of the other men. They were equally impressed with what they found and each in turn shook Stoner's hand in silent appreciation for all he had done to bring them here.

They managed to clear some of the land, enough to get them a small head start with the planting come spring. The downed trees just needed to be moved with a team of oxen to make way for the plow. They each included a flat, sheltered place to build their first homes.

The onslaught of winter stopped their labours and they headed back to Fort Erie along the trail they had come up a month before. Their mood was cheerful despite the driving sleet that dogged their every step.

With the coming of spring the settlers raced against time to get on the land. Tents were pitched as temporary shelters while the men finished clearing the land for cultivation.

Stoner swung the broad axe and felt it bite into the great trunk sending chips flying in every direction. The tree groaned in protest

before falling to the earth with a crash. The younger boys immediately swarmed over it, stripping the smaller branches and bundling them up for burning. Abraham Neff maneuvered the oxen into position to drag the log to the pile being assembled in the centre of the clearing. This was the last one for this field. They now had to haul and lever the logs into a pile to be burned.

Even as the men pushed and bullied the logs, the older boys started the plowing, weaving their way between the freshly cut stumps. Five years down the road they would be rotten enough to pull, but, in the meantime they would sow and reap among them. The younger children followed with the seed. The birds eagerly pounced on the grubs and insects churned up by the plow. They had a terrible knack of slipping behind the sowers to snatch up the seeds if not watched closely.

This scene was repeated on the farms of all three families. Log cabins were built, barns raised and meals cooked in a commu-

nal effort that assured the success of the fledgling community.

The Stoners, Neffs and Knisleys prospered in this virgin land. Their letters back to Lancaster County led to a great migration of Mennonite farmers to Upper Canada. Among the many families who settled in the southern part of the peninsula were the Sherks who came in large numbers before the turn of the 19th century.

HISTORICAL NOTE: The land occupied by Christian Stoner eventually was surveyed and consisted of parts of lots 29, 30, 31 and 32 in the third concession of Humberstone Township. This property today is bounded on the north by the Third Concession, on the south by Barrick Road, on the east by Elm Street and extends over Highway 58 (Westside Road) on the west. The subdivision that includes Apollo and Gemini Streets; Hillcrest, Runnymede and Thorncrest Roads; Oxford Boulevard, Windsor Terrace and Park Lane are all part of this original grant to Christian Stoner.

CHAPTER TWELVE
THE HUNGRY YEAR

About the time that Christian Stoner was settling his land in Humberstone a sergeant in Butler's Rangers by the name of Jacob Dittrick was applying for a land grant of his own. Since the disbanding of the rangers he had been working a farm between Queenston and Niagara owned by Captain John MacDonell.

The Dittricks were of German descent. Jacob's grandfather was from the Palatine region of Germany. They had settled in the Mohawk Valley of New York State about thirty miles from Utica in 1710.

With the outbreak of the American Revolution most of the Palatines remained loyal to Britain. They had fled persecution in their native land and found freedom and tolerance under British rule. In contrast they noted a certain degree of bigotry in the new republicanism of their rebel neighbours. After a number of close calls with the local committee of public Safety, Jacob made his way to Fort Niagara and enlisted in the rangers.

Jacob went on many raids with the rangers, sometimes into his old haunts in the Mohawk Valley. He was able to repay the rebels for the indignations suffered by his family in the early stages of the war.

Jacob became friendly with another ranger, William Pickard, whose family was among the refugees at Fort Niagara. Pickard's daughter, Margaret, caught Jacob's eye and a romance soon flourished amid the squalid conditions of the camp. After a brief courtship they married in late 1779 or early 1780.

While the men were away fighting Margaret lived with her mother in a cabin on Four Mile Creek on the east bank of the river. Days were spent worrying and watching for the return of the company from another foray deep into enemy territory.

In the tiny cabin, on October 9 1780, Margaret gave birth to their first child, a daughter. They named her Catherine. A son Robert was born January 20, 1783 at the same place.

While Jacob was working the MacDonnell

farm their second son, James, was born on August 29, 1785. Jacob named his son after James Secord, a lieutenant in the rangers whom he had greatly admired during the war.

In 1787 Jacob obtained a grant of four hundred acres on the Twelve Mile Creek and began clearing the land. With the help of his new neighbours his stump studded acreage was ready for the spring planting. No sooner had he sown the fields with seed then disaster struck. The winter of 1787-88 was a dry one and the coming of spring offered no relief. The rain held off and the newly planted crops withered in the fields. To make matters worse the government had cut off the rations that had sustained the settlers for the previous three years. The summer of 1788 through the summer of 1789 became known as The Hungry Year.

Jacob stood surveying his parched field of corn or, what should have been corn. The ground was a patch quilt of cracks and the stunted plants rustled in the dust kicked up by the hot winds. Where the stocks of the newly sprouted corn should have been whispering in the breeze, the crackling sound of dried leaves greeted his ears instead.

Jacob had just come from Fort Niagara where he had gone in search of food. The garrison had been able to spare him a little flour and a few potatoes, but, these would not go far.

His wife, Margaret, was out digging for eatable roots on the edge of the forest while the two older children tried their luck fishing in the Twelve Mile Creek. He worried about them all. Margaret was expecting their fourth child and the lack of good food was beginning to show, although she did not complain.

The children were showing signs of malnutrition as well and it was at times like these that they were the most vulnerable to sickness. Madeline Secord had stopped by two days earlier after attending to a sick child near DeCew Falls. The child had fallen into

the water and caught a chill. Normally this might have passed without incident, but, weakened by the lack of food, the boy died in his mother's arms the following day.

Jacob eyed the family dog who was scrounging for scraps where none were to be found. The poor beast was starving along with rest of them. Jacob had heard of dogs being used for food in the west. Indeed some Canadian voyageurs were said to consider them a delicacy. At that moment he made his decision and that night the family ate their first meat in three weeks.

Margaret gave birth to a daughter on the fourth of October 1788. Jacob insisted that she be called Margaret after her mother who had come through her confinement so bravely. Margaret's recovery was slow, aggravated by the scarcity of food. Jacob made another decision he had been dreading for weeks. He slaughtered his horse to be certain that the family would have a chance to survive the coming winter. The spring plowing took second place to the well being of his family.

The winter of 1789 returned to normal and the spring brought the reassuring patter of rain to the rooftops. Although it would be a hungry summer, if they could hold out until the harvest, all would be well again. Between the spring runoff and the warming rain, the earth again gave up its bounty to the pioneers of the Peninsula.

Jacob Dittrick and his family prospered. After the year of drought the land lived up to the promise Jacob had seen as it was being cleared.

The family grew as well. Margaret gave birth to Jacob Jr., February 12, 1791; Walter, May 31, 1793; William, December 20, 1795; Jaminia, March 12, 1799; George, December 20, 1801; Rebecca, October 23, 1803; and Caroline, November 20, 1807.

CHAPTER THIRTEEN
BATTLING THE GRIM REAPER

Madeline Secord awoke with a start, disoriented by being snapped out of a deep sleep. As she subconsciously shrugged off the shroud of mist that enveloped her, she realized that it was the pounding at the door that had awakened her. She stumbled to the door and fumbled with the latch. As the door sprang open the cold night air rushed upon her probing for weaknesses in the tightly clutched robed that warded off their assault.

"Mrs. Secord?" A shy voice inquired out of the darkness. Madeline quickly lit a lamp motioning to the voice to come in as she did so. It was Robert Hamilton's stable boy.

'What is it, Jeremiah?" She asked.

"Mr. Robert sent me to fetch you, ma'am," he stammered, "There's a woman havin' a baby at the landing and she's carryin' on somethin' awful." Without a word Madeline dressed and ventured out into the crisp early morning air. The grass tips gleamed white in the eerie, predawn light.

Madeline heard the woman's screams long before she came in sight of the landing. On reaching the tent where she was confined she told the boy to wait in case she needed him.

Madeline would not soon forget those cries and the scene that greeted her. She could not tell if the woman was young or old. She was bathed in sweat and from the look of her hair and the surrounding bedding she had been in labour for many hours. Madeline quickly went to work probing and feeling. After a brief examination she looked at the other women, but she could see that she did not have to tell them the prognosis.

She sat with the woman through the day listening to screams that were punctuated by periods of blessed unconsciousness. The affair ended in an arrested labour and both mother and child died.

Madeline stepped from the tent and glanced at the sky noting that it was close to supper time. She wiped her hands on her apron and looked at the dejected young man sitting with his head in his hands.

The young couple were loyalists who had been forced to flee their home in Upper New York State. They had shuffled from one place to another despite the advanced stage of the woman's pregnancy. They had camped near the landing after crossing the Niagara the day before and sometime in the night she had gone into labour. Madeline felt sorry for the young man and she suddenly realized that she didn't even know his name.

Childbirth was a dangerous time for both mother and child in the 1790s. Arrested labour, caused when the baby's head was too large relative to the mother's pelvis, was one cause of death to mother and child. The young woman that Madeline Secord had attended probably suffered from rickets as a child with the subsequent distortion to the pelvic bones. Consequently an otherwise normal baby was unable to deliver.

Puerperal Fever was another cause of death to new mothers in Upper Canada. We now know that Puerperal Fever was a result of Streptococcal invading the uterus at the time of birth. After what seemed to be an uneventful delivery, the mother would mysteriously take ill and die some two or three days later.

Although the danger of infection was always nearby, not all childbirths were difficult. Most deliveries were fairly routine. Babies were usually delivered by midwives who were neighbours with no formal training other than having gone through the ordeal themselves. Doctors were few and far between in the Niagara of the 1790s.

Even after a normal delivery the child was not out of the woods. Only half of newborns lived to see their fifth birthday. Many diseases lay in wait for the pioneer child. Scarlet Fever, Whooping Cough, and Diphtheria were among the deadly illnesses that struck without warning sometimes in epidemic proportions. It was not uncommon for several children from the same family to die within a few days of one another. Even the common childhood diseases such as measles, chicken pox and mumps had a high mortality rate.

A letter written by Hannah Jarvis to Rev. S. Peters in 1803 will give some insight into the problem: " . . . Maria was at the point of death with the measles. I believe no one ever recovered at so dangerous a situation before . . . for five day(s) she was unable to lay down for a moment (she) sat at the side of the bed . . . three weeks was I without once taking off my clothes . . . This poor child the moment she missed me would call out mama . . . I had nine down at once with that fatal disorder."

Tuberculosis was another disease that began to take hold in Upper Canada. In those days it was referred to as consumption and many children succumbed to this disease.

Teething was another time of concern in a child's life. Often children died of the fevers associated with it. In the days before modern remedies such things had to run their course.

It is hard to comprehend the possibility of losing half your children before they reached the age of five. Indeed five was not a magic number. It was not unusual to lose children who were near their teens.

This leads us to wonder about the attitude towards children in those days. One father described his reaction to the death of his six year old son this way: "And nothing teaches us better not to spoil them and love them too much, regrets are less intense."

There is nothing to support a claim that parents always succeeded in tempering their love for their children. Elizabeth Simcoe, wife of John Graves Simcoe, wrote after the death of her fifteen month old daughter at Niagara: "She was the sweetest tempered, pretty child imaginable, just beginning to talk and walk and the suddenness of the event you may be sure shocked me inexpressibly . . . the recollection of the loss of so promising a child must long be a painful thing."

NOTE: Much of the material for this "Niagara Story" was gleaned from a paper entitled: "Children, From the Womb to the Tomb; The struggle for Health During Upper Canada's First Generation," presented at the 1984 Niagara Peninsula History Conference at Brock University by Dr. Charles G. Roland, M.D.

CHAPTER FOURTEEN
SIMCOE: THE FATHER OF UPPER CANADA

While the pioneers in the Peninsula struggled through the Hungry Year, events in far off London were falling into place that would profoundly affect Niagara. The fate of Canada and the American Loyalists was debated in Parliament and in the streets of the British capital.

John Graves Simcoe had distinguished himself during the American Revolution. He commanded the Queen's Rangers, a corps of loyal Americans, who fought much as Butler's Rangers did, as raiders. At the end of hostilities Simcoe returned to England to recover from wounds. During his convalescence he worried about the fate of the loyalists he had left behind.

To further his ability to influence the shape of Canada and to provide a refuge for American loyalists, he entered parliament in 1790. He championed Canada as, "A place of value to the crown with a future in the commercial affairs of the world."

At this time the whole of Canada was called Quebec and subject to French civil law and land holding customs. To give British settlers, especially loyalists, the right to live under British law and its free hold system he proposed dividing the colony into two parts, Lower and Upper Canada. An order-in-council dated 24 August, 1791 brought his dream to a reality. Simcoe was even given the opportunity to see his dream through when he was appointed the first Lieutenant Governor of Upper Canada.

Simcoe had some definite ideas about the structure of this new colony. The city of Kingston had ambitions of being the capital of Upper Canada, in fact, Lord Dorchester had promised the citizens that it would be. However, Simcoe squelched that notion almost immediately. He was determined to establish his capital in the centre of the territory. He wrote: "For the purposes of Commerce, Union and Power, I propose that the site of the colony should be in that Great Peninsula between the Lakes Huron, Erie and Ontario, a spot designed by nature, sooner or later, to govern the interior world. I mean to establish a capital in the heart of the country, upon the River Thames . . ." Simcoe's capital ultimately did not fall on the River Thames, but in the Niagara Peninsula.

Simcoe arrived in Quebec on November 11, 1791 and wintered there. The following spring he moved on to Kingston where he took his oath of office and prepared for the job ahead. On July 26, 1792 the ship, Onondaga, anchored in the mouth of the Niagara River and Newark (Niagara-on-the-Lake) became the first capital of Upper Canada.

Elizabeth Simcoe stood outside the marquee that had been set up as temporary accommodations while the renovations to Navy Hall were being completed. She had to concede that it was an inauspicious beginning for a capital. It boasted a half dozen houses of indifferent quality and even the wooden barracks used by the navy would pass for little better than a carriers' ale-house in England. There was a bright spot, however. Soon various government officials would build fine homes and transform it into a thriving community.

Her gaze wandered down into the town, and she had to admit that the houses looked much better at a distance. She was determined to sketch them from her present vantage point. Behind her a meadow stretched out to a wood that one of the garrison officers had told her contained a good road leading to the great falls of which she had heard so much. Directly ahead of her was an unobstructed view of the river and of Fort Niagara on the American side.

Monday morning found Elizabeth in a state of great excitement for they were going off to see the Falls of Niagara that lay some sixteen miles to the south. At eight o'clock she stepped into a caleche and settled down beside her husband for the drive to the West Landing where they were to breakfast with Robert Hamilton, a merchant and member of the executive council, before continuing on to the falls.

Robert Hamilton greeted his guests with all

the ceremony that could be mustered in the village of Queenston in 1792. By any standard he was a very prosperous man. He was one of the contractors on the Portage Road as well as having warehouses and a mercantile business in the village. His was the finest house in the region. After a sumptuous breakfast the Simcoe entourage headed out for the falls.

The Simcoes stood in awe of the breathtaking view of the thundering cataract. Elizabeth insisted on climbing down the steep hill to Table Rock, sketch book in hand, to experience the power of the falls first hand. She gazed at the Grand Falls with its circular shape and green colour along with the great plume of spray that reached skyward. One of the staff officers pointed out the Montmorency Falls that was separated from the Grand Falls by a large island. A few rocks stood between it and the Fort Schlosser Falls that, unlike its larger cousin, fell over a straight ledge of rock. As they watched a large rainbow appeared in the mist of the Grand Falls.

The party went on to Fort Chippawa where Simcoe inspected the troops and the fortifications. Darkness overtook them on their return and they spent the night at Robert Hamilton's house at the West Landing.

The Simcoes stayed at Niagara for a three years before the capital was moved to York. John Graves Simcoe left an indelible mark on Upper Canada when he left in 1796. He divided the districts into counties in 1792 bringing Lincoln County into existence. The county covered much of what became Lincoln, Welland, Wentworth and Haldimand Counties. The foundation for the future of the Niagara Peninsula was laid.

HISTORICAL NOTE: The names given the falls in this account are those familiar to the Simcoes. The Grand Falls is the Horseshoe Falls, the Montmorency, the Bridal Veil and the Fort Schlosser, the American.

CHAPTER FIFTEEN
THE FIRST PARLIAMENT OF UPPER CANADA

John Graves Simcoe, more than any other Lieutenant Governor to follow him, held a vision of Canada spawned by a genuine interest in the country and its inhabitants. He had been posted to America as a young subaltern at the outbreak of the War for American Independence. At his own request he was given command of the Queen's Rangers, made up of loyalists from New York and Connecticut. He fought throughout the war with his regiment before returning to England in 1781.

Through his American service Simcoe was convinced that the American Revolution was a conspiracy of a minority of the population. Many people in the United States were fundamentally still loyal to Britain in his view. The republican government to the south was unstable and corrupt and he felt that, with a government on the British model with a "pure administration of its laws," many Americans would rally to the Empire.

Simcoe planned to make Upper Canada a miniature England, a reflection of British institutions and customs. To this end he began by changing the names of Towns and rivers to those of England. In the peninsula Chippawa Creek became the Welland River and Niagara became Newark. In naming new places he followed the same pattern. When he divided the province into counties the names of the townships in Lincoln County were names found in Lincolnshire in England. Louth, Stamford and Grantham are examples of this.

Simcoe was determined to keep hostile American influences away from Upper Canada, however, he wished to attract that vast majority of Americans he thought to be, at least, passively loyal to the crown to settle in the country. To achieve his goal a system of land grants was established as the townships were surveyed. He sent a letter to the British consul in Philadelphia outlining the advantages of Upper Canada to emigrants from Pennsylvania. He was particularly anxious to attract Quakers offering them an exemption from bearing arms if they would settle in the province.

Despite being stationed in the backwoods of Canada Simcoe insisted on the proper decorum and pageantry associated with British rule. At the opening of the first parliament at Newark in 1792 the honour guard was made up of his old Regiment, the Queen's Rangers. Resplendent in their scarlet tunics, they formed up at Navy Hall to be inspected by the Lieutenant Governor. While the inspection went on the naval vessels in the harbour fired a royal salute and the military band played "God Save the King."

The first session went well by Simcoe's estimation despite the make up of the assembly. He was an aristocrat and was shocked to find that many members of the legislature kept one table. That is, their servants ate at the same table with the family. This was not the type of aristocracy that he had envisioned for Upper Canada.

Although Simcoe was a conservative and a firm believer in tradition, he was not above making concessions to the weather. The summer of 1793 was a particularly hot and humid one. At the parliamentary session held at Newark that year the members met and transacted the government's business under a huge oak tree. The tree became known as Parliament Oak and lived until the late 1960s. A school now sits on the site called, appropriately, Parliament Oak School.

Today, we would probably consider Simcoe a snob and he was that. But, he did have a true sense of justice and human rights that were ahead of his time. The second session of the parliament debated and passed a bill calling for the gradual abolition of slavery. Simcoe had pressed for a total ban on the practice, but several legislators had brought their Negro slaves with them from the south and were reluctant to lose their cheap labour. Simcoe compromised and the law allowed for slaves already in the province to remain such for the rest of their lives. However, no new slaves could be introduced into the province and children born to female slaves were to be freed on reaching their twenty-fifth birthday.

Simcoe toured the province extensively. In

February and March of 1793 he went to Detroit and on the way confirmed his earlier thought that the capital of the province should be at the confluence of the branches of the Thames River where the city of London now stands. At the time, however, its location was not practical due to the lack of roads and settlements. He was determined to build a military road from Burlington Bay to the Thames and in the summer a contingent of the Queen's Rangers began the road that was called Dundas Street after the Secretary of State.

Simcoe next journeyed to Lake Aux Claies north of Toronto. He renamed the little village York and the lake he named Lake Simcoe in honour of his father. He traveled to Georgian Bay via the Severn River and returned to York by the same route. He immediately ordered a survey made to build a road from York to Lake Simcoe to provide rapid communications with the upper lakes in case of war with the United States. In 1796 this road was built using the Queen's Rangers once again. This road was called Yonge Street after the

Secretary of War.

Simcoe did not spend all his time looking internally at Upper Canada. He focused some of his attention on the United States. He watched as the Americans slowly drove the western Indians from their traditional hunting grounds. In 1791 the Indians had defeated the American attempt to push them west, however, in 1793 Anthony Wayne led a campaign that defeated the Indians at Fallen Timbers. This brought the Americans into close proximity to the British garrison at Fort Miami. Simcoe felt that war was inevitable, but the Americans withdrew after a brief show of force.

Simcoe left Canada in July of 1796, but he put his stamp on Upper Canada that succeeding administrators could not erase. He prepared the province and the Peninsula for the nineteenth century and the troubles and conflicts that were to come.

CHAPTER SIXTEEN
THE LIEUTENANT GOVERNOR'S LADY

John Graves Simcoe's tenure as Lieutenant Governor of Upper Canada left a lasting impression on the Niagara Peninsula. Another Simcoe also left her mark on pioneer settlements of our country. Elizabeth Posthuma Simcoe, the Lieutenant Governor's wife, had a vitality and personality that touched everyone that met her.

She was born in late September of 1762. Her father, Lieutenant Colonel Thomas Gwillim, was the commanding officer of the 50th Regiment of Foot and died while on active duty before Elizabeth was born. He had been a brigade-major under Wolfe at Quebec in 1759 and had remained in Canada until late 1761. The Gwillim's had been childless and he died not knowing that he was to be a father. Her mother, born Elizabeth Spincks, died giving birth to Elizabeth. In honour of her dead parents she was given the middle name Posthuma by her aunt and grandmother who raised her.

Elizabeth met John Graves Simcoe, ten years her senior, in December 1781. He stayed at Hembury Fort House, the home of her aunt and her husband Admiral Samuel Graves, who was Simcoe's godfather, to convalesce from wounds suffered in the American campaign. Part of Simcoe's routine was to take long walks to build up his strength and Elizabeth became his constant companion. They shared an interest in art and often took sketch pad and pencil on their outings.

They were married on the 30th of December 1782. In January of 1784 she gave birth to their first child, a girl whom they called Eliza. A second daughter was born in August of 1785 called Charlotte and in April 1787 another daughter, Henrietta Maria joined the family. She gave birth to two more girls before the decade was out.

1791 was a significant year for Elizabeth. Her husband was appointed Lieutenant Governor of Upper Canada, an appointment he coveted, and their son Francis was born. Leaving their four eldest daughters in England to be educated, the Simcoes sailed for Canada with their youngest daughter, Sophia and their infant son.

They arrived at Niagara in July of 1792 aboard the eighty ton topsail schooner "Onondaga" to view for the first time the place that was to become the first capital of Upper Canada. Elizabeth settled into life in Upper Canada with ease. To her this was a great adventure.

No house awaited the Simcoes on their arrival at Niagara. The town, which Simcoe renamed Newark only had a half dozen buildings that Elizabeth described as, "of indifferent quality."

Navy Hall, the government building, was in disrepair forcing them to make do with a number of tents that they had pitched overlooking the town and the river. Elizabeth was quite content with the arrangements and filled her days entertaining, sketching and writing in her journal.

Elizabeth was not above slipping out for a little adventure. In September of 1792 her husband left her at Fort Chippawa while he made an inspection trip to Long Point on Lake Erie. She wished to return to the Tice farm on Mountain Road in Stamford but had no man to take her. Despite having never driven a Caleche she strapped young Francis in and drove the Portage Road to her destination. She described it in her journal: "But having no gentleman with me I was obliged to drive the carriage myself, which I had never done, and the roads were excessively rough till after the falls. I tied Francis into the carriage and drove him very safely, Altho' he complained of being much bruised and shook."

Elizabeth gave birth to her seventh child on the 16th of January 1793. It was a girl that they named Katherine after Simcoe's mother Katherine Stamford. The winter of 1793 was a particularly harsh one. On February 27th Elizabeth endured the coldest day she had ever witnessed. She was staying with the family of Chief Justice Osgoode and the temperature in the house would not raise above fifty-five degrees, despite the stove

being red hot.

In April of 1794 tragedy struck the Simcoe household while they were at York. Katherine, their little girl, died. Elizabeth wrote back to England telling the rest of the family: "It is with pain I take up my pen to inform you of the loss we have sustained and the melancholy event of our losing poor little Katherine, one of the strongest, healthiest children you ever saw . . . She had been feverish one or two days cutting teeth, which not being an unusual case with children I was not much alarmed. On good Friday she was playing in my room in the morning, in the afternoon was seized with fits. I sat up the whole night the greatest part of which she continued to have spasms and before seven in the morning she was no more."Katherine was buried in the military cemetery near the huts of the Queen's Rangers, which Simcoe had named Fort York, on Easter Monday, 1794. A few days later Francis became ill and Elizabeth was in panic. Would she lose two children in such a short time? It was too common place in the area to be discounted. She sent for the surgeon in Newark but by the time he arrived Francis was well again and Elizabeth's fears were allayed.

Elizabeth spent part of 1794 at Quebec and returned to Upper Canada in February 1795. The journey was accomplished by sleigh, and she had some harrowing experiences crossing the ice as a number of rivers were beginning to thaw. After a lengthy stay in Kingston, the Simcoes arrived at York in May. They sailed for Newark aboard the "Onondaga" on the ninth of June stopping at Burlington Bay on their way. Elizabeth and the children settled into their tents for a summer of traveling up and down the peninsula. The Whirlpool was a particular favourite of Elizabeth and she went there often, crossing the Thompson farm to get to it, usually in a caleche.

1796 saw the end of the Simcoe's stay in Canada. They drove to Queenston to say goodbye to the Hamiltons. They stopped briefly at the Greens on Forty Mile Creek for they had enjoyed their hospitality on many occasions.

They set sail on September 10 aboard the "Pearl" and spent much of the voyage below decks because of pursuing French war ships. They landed at Dover on October 13 and Elizabeth rushed home to see the daughters she had left behind five years earlier. Elizabeth went about renewing her acquaintances in England and getting to know her own family once again.

John Graves Simcoe died in 1806 while preparing to go to India. Elizabeth lived to a ripe old age and died on January 17, 1850. She held a life long interest in Canada and followed events closely right up until the end of her life. She left as indelible a mark on the Peninsula as did her husband.

CHAPTER SEVENTEEN

THE REBEL & THE LOYALIST

The decision of two men of very diverse backgrounds were to have a momentous impact on the future of the Niagara Peninsula. One's son would alter the history of Upper Canada, the other would indirectly foster a legend.

Thomas Merritt was born and raised on a farm between Bedford and Long Island Sound in Westchester County, New York. At the outbreak of the American Revolution the Merritt family remained loyal to the crown. Thomas with his father, Thomas Senior, and brother escaped to the British lines and Thomas enlisted in the Queen's Rangers commanded by Colonel John Graves Simcoe. He was commissioned a coronet and saw action throughout the war. The Regiment was sent to the Southern Colonies and while there Thomas married Mary Hamilton of South Carolina. They took up residence near New York City shortly thereafter where they lived out the rest of the war. It was here that they lost their first born child shortly before the war ended in 1783.

When the Queen's Rangers were disbanded in 1783 the Merritts went north with the rest of the loyalists and settled in New Brunswick. Merritt Senior could not get a land grant and took up fishing, which he worked at until his death in 1821.

Thomas Junior's stay in New Brunswick was short. The cold winters were too much for Mary and they moved back to the fledgling United States settling near Mary's former home in South Carolina.

Life was rough for the former loyalists and, when Mary suffered a miscarriage, they moved north settling in Bedford, New York near the old Merritt family home. It was there on July 3, 1793 that a son was born to them. They named him William Hamilton, a name that was to have a profound affect on the history of this region.

Thomas Ingersoll was, in many respects, the opposite of Thomas Merritt. He lived in Great Barrington, Massachusetts and in 1775, at the age of twenty-six, married seventeen year old Elizabeth Dewey. In the same year a daughter was born to them whom they christened Laura. Laura Ingersoll was to become one of the legendary heroines of Upper Canada.

At the outbreak of the revolution Ingersoll was torn between the rebels and the British. Feelings against the crown ran particularly high in Massachusetts and in 1777 he joined the rebels and held a captaincy in the Massachusetts Militia.

With the war winding down in 1783 tragedy struck the Ingersoll household with the death of Thomas' young wife, Elizabeth, leaving him with four daughters to raise. A year later he remarried only to lose this second wife four years later. Within a few months he married Sarah Whiting who was eventually to give birth to four sons and three daughters bringing the Ingersoll family to a total of eleven children.

Ingersoll soon became disillusioned with the new republic. Times were chaotic in the years following the revolution and many patriots had second thoughts about the freedom they had fought for. The expression: "Switching one tyrant three thousand miles away for three thousand tyrants one mile away," was often true.

The generous terms offered to settlers in Upper Canada soon filtered down to Great Barrington, and Ingersoll and four partners drew up a petition asking Governor Simcoe for a township grant. Township grants were awarded to persons willing to commit to bringing a set number of settlers to the area within a specified period of time. Ingersoll traveled to Niagara to present the petition in person in March of 1793.

Thomas Ingersoll stepped from the Fairbanks Tavern, where he had spent the night, into the chill morning air. He had arrived the day before from the Landing on the American side of the Niagara River. He was still puzzled over the name of the village he was in. On the American side they referred to it as the West Landing, on this side he heard the name Queenstown as well as West Landing. When he inquired at the tavern as to the correct

designation he sparked a lively debate among the locals. Some said West Landing, others insisted that it was now Queen's Town, no it was Queenstown insisted others while the tavern keeper had it on good authority that the proper name was Queenston.

As he pondered these things the caleche that he had hired to take him to Newark arrived and he embarked for the ride to see Governor Simcoe. He saw a pleasant countryside as they made their way along the rutted road to the capitol. He was graciously received by the bureaucrats and his business was transacted quickly.

Thomas Ingersoll's petition was approved for a township grant on the Thames River called Oxford-Upon-the-Thames on the condition that he and his associates bring in a minimum of forty settlers within seven years. Each family was to receive two hundred acres for a nominal land fee. It was to be two years before Ingersoll could wind up his affairs and move his family.

While Thomas Ingersoll was successfully completing his business in Niagara, Thomas Merritt was also casting his eyes north. He wrote a letter to his old commanding officer, John Graves Simcoe, inquiring as to the availability of land in Upper Canada. He received a reply inviting him to settle in the province assuring him of a generous grant. In the summer of 1794 Merritt made the journey to Niagara to satisfy himself that this was indeed the promised land he had heard so much about.

Thomas Merritt approached Navy hall in Newark with some apprehension. It had been ten years since he had seen John Graves Simcoe. Simcoe had been a colonel then, what would his reaction be to his former subordinate now that he was Lieutenant Governor no less.

Thomas' worries were unfounded. Simcoe gave him a warm welcome and sat discussing old campaigns and new beginnings telling Thomas that a great future awaited him in this land of opportunity. He did not meet Mrs. Simcoe as they had just lost their youngest child, Katherine.

Merritt said his farewells determined to move his family to the Niagara Peninsula. That decision was to have a far reaching affect on all of us.

CHAPTER EIGHTEEN
WHERE ON EARTH IS BROWN'S BRIDGE?

About the time that Ingersoll and Merritt were considering settling in Niagara an old soldier was contemplating his future on the Chippawa Creek west of the Seven Mile Stake. John Brown took up residence at Niagara after the Revolutionary War in the 1780s.

Brown had seen action at the Battle of the Plains of Abraham as a lieutenant in the British Army in 1759. He recalled most vividly the sight of General James Wolfe directing the battle, encouraging the troops. Brown had seen blood dripping from Wolfe's right hand and that he was holding his stomach with his left as blood seeped between his fingers. Wolfe ordered the charge and, though twice wounded, ran forward with the rest. It was then that he sagged to his knees, a ball in his chest. Brown helped carry him to the rear and cradled him as he lay dying from his wounds. Brown quickly rejoined his regiment, the 60th, and was severely wounded himself.

In 1760 Brown returned to Ireland where he married Agnes Glaise. In 1770 they immigrated to America where they settled in New Jersey. At the outbreak of the American Revolution Brown joined the British forces and moved north with other loyalists at the end of the war.

After a number of years in the northern part of the peninsula, he decided to try his luck on new land along the Chippawa Creek in Thorold Township. In 1788 he packed up his family and together with his long time servants Abraham and Lydia Lee, two former slaves, began the journey over rough roads and trails to Thorold. He set up camp on the banks of the Chippawa at the foot of present day Pelham Street. The long arduous task of carving out a homestead in the wilderness stood before him.

Brown cleared the land and built a house with the help of the Lees and his three sons. The following year he made contact with his neighbours to the south, among them Christian Stoner and the other Mennonites who were beginning to settle in Humberstone Township. The Chippawa proved to be a formidable obstacle in communicating with them and the fledgling community that was building around the Sugar Loaf. Brown decided that a bridge across the river would give him ready access to mills and supplies as well as toll income from traffic going to the Short Hills and beyond.

The bridge was constructed of timber pilings and a plank decking. With this route opened things looked rosy for the Browns when tragedy struck. John Brown contracted smallpox and died in 1795. He had applied for a land grant of six hundred and fifty acres in that same year. His wife filed for a further grant of three hundred acres in 1796. With the help of the Lees and her children she was able to continue farming after his death.

A bustling community grew up around the bridge on the north side aptly named Brown's Bridge. One of the first schools was built here, the Union Section Number Two School, which doubled as a meeting house on the Thorold side of the town line.

During the War of 1812 orders were given to burn the bridges over the Chippawa to slow the enemy. Misener's Bridge to the east was torched, but for some reason Brown's Bridge was spared.

Brown's Bridge almost figured in the plans for the first Welland Canal. In 1823 Mr. Hiram Tibbet surveyed several routes, one of which he reported: "Commenced at Chippawa on the 6th Inst. 10 miles from its mouth as stated by me, on Mr. John Brown's farm, Township of Thorold, explored two routes from thence to the headwaters of the 12 Mile Creek."

In 1824 the first library in the area, called the Welland Library Company, was set up at the school at Brown's Bridge. Some of the available books were: Adam Smith's *Wealth of Nations,* Paley's *Philosophy* and Washington's *Official Letters.*

The first anniversary meeting of the board was held at the school on November 26, 1825. Among the shareholders present was Alexander Brown, son of John Brown. At the meeting the constitution was discussed, and it

might be of some interest to see how libraries of the day operated. The bylaws concerning the borrowing of books were as follows: Books were borrowed for one month except in the case of someone living five miles from the library or greater. They could keep the book an extra week. The fine for overdue books was 7 1/2 pence. Other fines were levied as follows:

1) For folding down a leaf- 3 3/4 p

2) For every spot of grease- 3 3/4 p

3) For every torn leaf- 3 3/4 p

4) Any person allowing a library book to be taken out of his house paid a fine of five shillings. In 1858 this library was amalgamated with the Mechanics Institute of Welland.

Brown's Bridge continued to serve the Village of Welland until 1868 when, badly in need of extensive repairs, it was dismantled leaving the pilings to await another bridge that never came. Five of the pilings from Brown's Bridge can still be seen at low water after almost two hundred years, silent witnesses to the history of our peninsula.

Go down to the foot of Pelham Street at dusk when its quiet. Sit on the bank of the river and listen to the whisper of the pilings as they tell their tales of bygone days. Oh, and don't be surprised if you hear the clomp of horses hooves and the clatter of wagon wheels on the plank decking of Brown's bridge.

HISTORICAL NOTE: John Brown was present on the plains of Abraham, but there is some dispute whether he was at Wolfe's side when he died. Some attribute that honour to one Lieutenant Henry Browne.

CHAPTER NINETEEN
A JOURNEY TO EDEN

Thomas Ingersoll loaded his family into the wagon for the journey from Great Barrington to the Hudson River some twenty-five miles away. With his wife Sarah and eleven children he was setting out to build a new life in Upper Canada. The trip to the Hudson took the better part of a day, and he was thankful that they had relatives to spend the night with before boarding a sloop for the trip to Albany. From Albany a bone jarring, ten mile, wagon ride awaited them to Schenectady, New York.

The next part of the journey took them up the Mohawk Valley by Durham boat, a flat bottomed barge that was propelled by oars or poles against the strong current. A short portage found them on the Oswego River for the run down to the port of Oswego.

After a harrowing voyage by schooner to Niagara the Ingersolls landed and proceeded to Queenston where Thomas intended to settle his family while he went to Oxford Township to claim his land and build a house. He purchased a tavern in Queenston to give his family an income until the farm could begin to support them.

Throughout this, his eldest daughter Laura helped with the little ones and worked in the family business. At twenty years of age it was time for Laura to think about a suitable husband. She did not have far to look.

James Secord was the twenty-two year old son of James and Madeline Secord, among the first to settle in the Peninsula. James senior passed away suddenly in the winter of 1784 leaving James and his brothers to run the family farm.

The local Masonic Lodge began meeting at Ingersoll's inn in 1796, and James joined in that year. James looked forward to the lodge meetings on the chance that he might see the innkeeper's lovely daughter. He made every excuse to go calling on the Ingersolls and a budding romance grew over long walks in the village.

The following year Ingersoll was preparing to take his family to the homestead on the Thames and the thought of being separated decided the issue. James and Laura were married in 1797 taking up residence in St. Davids. James tended his farm and worked at the mercantile business that he had set up there.

Thomas Ingersoll moved his family to lot 20 in Oxford Township shortly after the marriage, leaving his daughter to her new life. Little did he realize how famous she would become.

While Thomas Ingersoll was getting his family settled at Queenston, Thomas Merritt was preparing to move his family from Bedford, New York to the Peninsula. In 1796, armed with a map showing available land, he set out with his wife and children, one of whom was three year old Hamilton. Merritt followed the same route that Ingersoll used a year earlier. Upon landing, Merritt discovered the colony in a state of confusion. The capital was in the process of moving from Newark to York and government clerks were stuck with things packed for the move, misplaced documents and others in transit. One thing was clear, however, all the good land along the Niagara was taken.

Thomas was in time to see the departure of his old commanding officer, John Graves Simcoe, who was going back to England. Simcoe tried to talk Merritt into taking free land near the new capital on the north shore of Lake Ontario, but he was determined to settle in Niagara. The best land available was along the Twelve Mile Creek, but was for purchase only. Merritt bought two hundred acres and was bent on becoming a farmer having grown tired of the mercantile business that had been his livelihood in New York.

For all the hardships of being on an isolated farm, miles from nowhere, Thomas Merritt was more than pleased with his circumstances. This was, for him, the finest country on earth. The Merritt's isolation was short lived, however, as settlers began pouring into Grantham Township.

The year after the Merritts took up their land George Adams built a tavern on the Twelve along a rudimentary road that ran on

to Burlington Heights. Adam's tavern was soon acquired by Paul Shipman and the small settlement that grew up there became known as Shipman's Corners. It soon became an important crossroad for traffic moving from Queenston and Newark to other parts of the Peninsula.

Local merchants from Newark and Queenston began coming to the area to offer their services. One such visitor to Thomas Merritt was Daniel Servos who came extolling the virtues of his complex at Palatine Hill. Servos still had the best milling facilities in the area and the long trek to his complex was worth the effort.

Thomas Merritt was well satisfied with the harvest. He was sending one of the servant girls to Palatine Hill to have the wheat ground into flour. As was the custom, with the narrow, rough roads, the grain was packed in sacks and slung over the backs of horses. As the girl was about to head off Thomas made a decision. Yes, it would do him good

to see the ways of the world even at his tender years. He called his five year old son, Hamilton, and sent him with the servant to Palatine Hill with the crop.

The servant girl smiled to herself. Master William Hamilton Merritt, five years old, felt himself to be in charge of this expedition and she decided to play along. She had no doubt that he would be a force to be reckoned with some day.

HISTORICAL NOTES: The lot on which Thomas Ingersoll settled his family in Oxford Township is located where the present day town of Ingersoll is situated. The land deal that Ingersoll had made with the government lapsed because the required number of settlers had not appeared. Ingersoll opened an inn on the Credit River in 1805 called Government House where he died in 1812.

Shipman's Corners was located at the corner of Ontario and St. Paul Streets in the City of St. Catharines

READING, RITING AND RITHMETIC

School was a hit and miss affair in the early part of the nineteenth century . There were no attendance laws and education played second fiddle to helping with the chores around the farm. If the district was fortunate, a woman agreed to teach reading and writing in her home for a small fee. Often they sat once or twice a week and attendance depended on the work load at home.

On school days the children were out before sun up to complete their chores. School was an exciting time as it gave the children a rare occasion to mix with their peers. Life on an isolated farm was a lonely affair. When the chores were done they climbed up on the plow horse and headed off to the neighbour's home that served as their school house. This "neighbour" might be several miles away. Many a young lad rode off to school with the admonition from his mother, "that a man who couldn't read or write would never amount to much."

The government was not too concerned about the education of the bulk of the population. Their primary objective was to establish grammar schools to train the future leaders of society. Even in a society struggling in the wilderness a distinct class structure left no doubt where those leaders would come from.

John Strachan, future Anglican bishop of Toronto and one of the leaders of the Family Compact, opened his "School for the Sons of Gentlemen" at Cornwall in 1804. In 1799 he ran a private school for the children of Richard Cartwright. The push for better schools came from settlers from the United States who, like the Merritts, emigrated in the late 1790s. Such settlers, used to the schools back home, were appalled by the lack of education in Upper Canada. Smith Hinman, whose family came to the province from New England in 1799, wrote years later: "The lack of schools and other privileges . . . was felt most keenly by them as their children were of an age to require schooling and society. . . . My father always thought that his father made a mistake in moving into this country."

One of the first schools in Niagara was opened in 1796 under the direction of one Rev. Arthur. The subjects taught were Reading, English Grammar, Writing, Arithmetic, Latin, Greek, Geography and Mathematics. Tuition was based on the number of subjects taken. These early schools were boarding schools as students came from great distances to study.

These schools often offered night classes for the locals. Many people who could afford the tuition were prevented from coming in the daytime because of their duties at home.

When the district could afford to hire a teacher for their common school he was paid the handsome sum of six dollars per year per student. In addition he received free room and board from a local family. To spread the burden he often stayed with several families throughout the year.

An early pioneer described the typical school at the turn of the nineteenth century this way: "Our first school was built of logs and had two rows of desks, one on each side facing the windows and placed against the walls. There were two rows of benches without backs for seats for the scholars. They were placed so high from the floor that the feet of the younger children dangled in the air. At one end of the room was the master's desk, table and chair. In the middle was a big boxstove with a bench on each side on which the children collected at recess or before school hours. There was no such things as blackboards, maps or globes and quill pens were used exclusively for writing. Part of the master's work was to see that the children's pens were kept properly mended."

Discipline in the schools was harsh. The schoolmaster used a birch rod, a cane or a strap to punish an offender. The usual method was to have the unfortunate individual bend over a desk where he was "caned" across the buttocks. It was often impossible to sit down after punishment.

It was not until 1816 that the government passed the Common School Act, which encouraged people to go to school. The act

provided that when a community built a schoolhouse and could undertake to supply it with twenty students, they could elect three trustees and hire a teacher. When the teacher taught for six months and received a certificate of acceptable service from the trustees, he could apply for his portion of the funds provided by the act. His pay depended on the number of students; however, it was not to exceed $100.00.

William Hamilton Merritt began his formal education in 1799 with the opening of a log school house at Shipman's Corners. The opportunities to learn at this school were limited, and Hamilton, as he was called by the family, was soon sent off to Ancaster to Richard Cockerell, one of the leading educators in Upper Canada.

Hamilton's life at Ancaster was an exciting one for a boy of nine. His father had given him a pony and he delighted in exploring the country around him, planting the seeds for his future interests.

It was not long before Mr. Cockerell moved his school to Newark to be closer to the centre of things. Although the capital was now at York, Newark and the surrounding district was considered an important military, legal and trading centre. This opened some new avenues to young Merritt. He was able to add to his education with some additional studies in the classics from the local Presbyterian minister, Rev. Burns.

HISTORICAL NOTE: A fine example of an early school house can be seen at the Port Colborne Historical Museum.

CHAPTER TWENTY-ONE

THE ADVENTURES OF WILLIAM HAMILTON MERRITT

In the early nineteenth century, even more so than today, education was the measure of a man's ability to rise in society. There was a distinct class system. Those who ruled and those who were governed. The principle of one man, one vote smacked of republicanism and the disruptive influence of democracy. Thomas Merritt was determined that his son Hamilton would take his rightful place among the elite of the community. When he reached his fifteenth birthday Thomas decided that it was time for him to broaden his education and see something of the world beyond the Peninsula.

Thomas' brother, Nehemiah, was a prominent merchant in St. John, New Brunswick where he had settled after the American Revolution. Thomas had originally settled there as well before returning to the United States and subsequently to Niagara. It was to his brother that Thomas chose to send his son to further his education.

Hamilton adjusted his new top hat and his cravat while looking in the hall mirror. He was off on a great adventure that would take him beyond the insulated world of the Niagara. He felt like a man for the first time in his life. Calls from the porch pulled him from his musings and he went out into the still morning air. His father waited with the wagon and team to take him to Niagara to catch the schooner for Kingston. He endured the embarrassment of a tearful farewell from his mother and the envious looks of his siblings before bounding up into the seat beside his father. With a wave he was off to see the world.

At Niagara he met Colonel John Clark and James Secord who were also bound for Kingston. Despite his youth the two men welcomed his company for the voyage. Captain Simpson weighed anchor. The ship heeled over under a press of sail dashing out of the mouth of the Niagara, meeting the first rollers of Lake Ontario and throwing a plume of spray over the bow to celebrate being free of the land.

Hamilton spent much of his time on deck, *afraid of missing something in this wonderful world of cords and canvas. As the little schooner changed tack there were a few minutes of apparent chaos, with ropes squealing through blocks and shouted orders of "haul smartly there," and "belay." Soon, however, the ropes were once more neatly flaked awaiting the next call of, "all hands, all hands."*

Midway through their journey another schooner, close hauled, on the opposite tack was sighted. Hamilton stood in awe as the great white sails came hurtling toward them. He was sure that the ship would leave the water and fly at any moment. James Secord remarked that it was one of Robert Hamilton's schooners bound for Queenston.

At Kingston, Hamilton said goodbye to his companions and set off by bateaux for Montreal. He caught another schooner at Montreal for Trois Riviere where he was entertained by some friends of his father. He toured the fort and the cathedral and waited for another vessel to run him to Quebec.

With no ship sailing for Quebec young Merritt decided to hire a caleche to drive him along the St. Lawrence to his destination. Baptiste, the driver, seemed to know everyone in the countryside. They were greeted with waves and good cheer all the way to Quebec.

His Uncle Nehemiah met him, as promised, aboard his ship the "Lord Sheffield" loading a cargo for the West Indies. It would take Hamilton as far as Halifax where he and his uncle would continue their journey to St. John. Before they weighed anchor in Quebec, however, fate stepped in to widen Hamilton's experience beyond his wildest dreams.

One of the "Lord Sheffield's" officers turned out to be a drunken alcoholic and Nehemiah decided that Hamilton's education would be better served by a voyage on the "Lord Sheffield." Hamilton was signed on as the supercargo. His job was to attend to the inventory on board and transact any business while on the voyage.

After a brief stop in Halifax they set sail for the West Indies. Hamilton's introduction to the ocean was a rude one. A series of summer storms hit the Lord Sheffield a few days out from Halifax. At one point the battered vessel began to take on water and a load of lumber, secured on deck, was jettisoned to lighten the ship.

In the midst of the howling gale Hamilton's first thought was the paperwork that needed to be done as supercargo to account for the loss. He might drowned with the entire crew before the night was out, yet, the first thought that came to mind was paperwork. He laughed despite the danger. One of the crew that witnessed this soon told the story to his mess mates. "Cool as a shark's belly, that one. Looked that gale in the face and laughed."

Five weeks after sailing from Halifax the leaking Sheffield limped into Hamilton, Bermuda. Even here she almost ran aground by taking the wrong channel. Merritt was glad to be on terra firma again. The ill fated Sheffield was not done with them yet. In a hurricane she broke free from her moorings and went ashore where the authorities declared her unseaworthy. Hamilton was stranded for six weeks before he could book passage for New York. The fare was $50.00 and took only twelve days to complete. He was fortunate to find a vessel, the "Union" outbound for St. John and he sailed January 15, 1809. On arriving he was greeted by his uncles and his grandfather whom he hardly knew. They soon remedied that situation.

Although a little late, Hamilton began his studies. He took up bookkeeping, navigation, surveying, algebra and Latin. The following June he entered college where he studied trigonometry and the other sciences.

Hamilton became restless as the leaves began to change. He announced that he would be going home to the Twelve to begin a new chapter in the life of the Niagara.

CHAPTER TWENTY-TWO
<u>HOME IS WHERE THE HEART IS</u>

William Hamilton Merritt's yearning for home began to assail him in July of 1809, just after his sixteenth birthday. His diary entries for that month may be of some interest:

July 3rd- Birthday; sixteen years of age.

" 8th- Went strawberrying with a nice party- lots of fine girls; very delightful.

" 22nd- To church. Confirmed by the Bishop of Nova Scotia; about one hundred candidates; two thirds of them females.

" 24th- Uncle Nehemiah arrived from England, soon after which concluded to return to Niagara; spent time pleasantly until departure.

Hamilton decided to return home via New York as the place had intrigued him at the time of his trip from Bermuda the previous year. In October he booked passage on a ship, loaded with plaster, bound for that city. They sailed from St. John and stayed close into the coast taking shelter in harbour every night.

However, Merritt's luck with the sea had not changed. A gale sprang up and the ship went aground at Martha's Vineyard, a small island off the coast of Massachusetts. They were stuck there until a small schooner happened along and towed them off the bar.

They finally reached Shrogg's Neck, Long Island where his ship was delayed once again. He hailed a passing sloop and went on to the old family homestead at Byram where he spent several days with an aunt and uncle named Lyons. He passed the time there recounting his sailing adventures, after which all agreed that the romance of the sea was highly exaggerated.

He stopped in New York for a few days and reacquainted himself with the city, enjoying the entertainment and amusements available there. He searched for a steamer bound upriver to Albany, but there were none to be found. He finally hitched a ride on a trading boat headed that way and reached it in due course.

Albany was the bustling trading centre for all of Upstate New York. Merritt saw Indians of the Iroquois Confederacy mingle with fur traders, drummers and tinkers from all across the northern United States and Canada. Perhaps it was the frontier atmosphere that rekindled the adventurous spirit within Merritt. At any rate, he decided to buy a horse and finish his journey on horseback.

Fortunately, the weather remained balmy as Hamilton rode on to Batavia. After resting up he took the Cherry Valley Turnpike eventually leaving it and making his way to Lewiston.

Hamilton stood on the dock at Lewiston staring across at the wooded slope of Queenston Heights. Home! Before he could suppress it a lump came to his throat. Home, with all that it meant to a sixteen year old boy. He willed the ferry to hurry. The homestead on the Twelve awaited him, more splendid than any palace of any king in the world.

Merritt fought with his horse to get him aboard the scow. The gentle rocking of the boat made the animal skittish and it took a few moments to calm him down. Finally the ferry pushed off and began to crawl up the back eddy in preparation for the dash to the far shore. The oars rose and dipped like the legs of some great water bug moving against the current.

At the top of their run they slowed, just holding the boat in place as they swung the bow toward the opposite shore. At a signal from the stern the oarsmen came alive, driving the blades in the water in a mad rush to beat the current to the dock slightly down river from them. Hamilton spoke softly to his horse, reassuring him that all was well.

They landed without incident and Hamilton, despite his rush to get home, stopped for lunch at the local tavern and paid his respects to the family of Robert Hamilton. He was saddened to hear of the death of Robert Hamilton that year and offered his condolences to the family.

After a brief stop in St. Davids, Hamilton headed for the Twelve and home. Approach-

ing the homestead along the split rail fence he raised his arm in a wave to the family who were completing chores in front of the house. All rushed up to greet him as he dismounted. Unlike when he left, he relished the attention and tears of his mother upon his return. He told tales of his adventures long into the night.

Merritt immediately looked for opportunities to put his education to good use. He saw that the village that was growing up around Shipman's Corners was in need of a general store. He went into partnership with William Chisholm and began to put his bookkeeping into practice. Money was scarce and much of the business was carried on in barter. Goods were paid for with ashes, pork, staves, honey, hides, grain and fruit. These were shipped to Montreal in payment for goods received by the store.

Merritt remained in the mercantile business for a couple of years until he sold his share to return to the homestead to run the family farm. His father was sheriff of Niagara and had little time to tend to the livestock and crops. As he approached his eighteenth birthday events were to change his life forever.

Hamilton chatted amiably with the young men and women at the church social. He was pointing out the attributes of a good horse when someone touched his shoulder. It was his mother who wished to introduce him to Doctor Jedediah Prendergast and his family who had come to the Peninsula from the United States. The ever gracious Hamilton was fine until introduced to the doctor's fair daughter Catherine. He was suddenly struck dumb much to the amusement of his siblings.

Hamilton quickly recovered his wits and after some awkward moments began a long conversation with her. They talked of sea adventures, education, home and myriad other interests that they shared. A firm friendship was born that day, which was to blossom into a budding romance.

By his eighteenth birthday Merritt had been to sea, been a successful merchant and managed a good sized farm. All pointed to a tranquil, successful future for him; however, events in far off places were to alter that future dramatically.

CHAPTER TWENTY-THREE

GROWTH ON THE PORTAGE ROAD

While William Hamilton Merritt was starting his career at the bustling community around Shipman's Corners other areas of the peninsula were thriving as well. On the road to Queenston was the village of St. Davids. David Secord was its leading citizen. Secord's grist mill on the Four Mile Creek was one of the earliest in the Peninsula, and he also owned a general store. In 1809 there were thirty to forty good houses in the village as well as blacksmith shops and several stores. Four Mile Creek was alive with saw mills and grist mills along its banks at St. Davids.

North on the Four Mile Creek Road was another village at the junction of Four Mile Creek Road and the Black Swamp Road (Niagara Stone Road). The early travelers, who stopped to refresh themselves and their horses, called it Four Mile Creek. The first official name was Crossroads and it later became known as Lawrenceville after George Lawrence one of its earliest citizens. It consisted of an inn and a few farm buildings.

Niagara (Newark, Niagara-on-the-Lake) continued to be the military and cultural capital of Upper Canada even though the official capital was now "Muddy" York. It boasted a library that dated from June of 1800 and many of its leading citizens were the movers and shakers of their day. William Dickson, kinsmen of Robert Hamilton of Queenston, was a successful merchant in Niagara and owned a fine house with an extensive private library, which was his pride and joy.

The village of Queenston rapidly out stripped Niagara in the world of business in the early nineteenth century. Robert Hamilton, a prominent merchant whose home was at Queenston, became one of the most influential men in Upper Canada. As a member of the Executive Council he often entertained John Graves Simcoe and his wife, Elizabeth, when they were stationed in Canada in the mid 1790's.

In 1790 Hamilton joined forces with several others including Thomas Clark to bid on the contract to operate the portage from Queenston to Chippawa. They had been operating the route since 1788 in anticipation of the relinquishing of the east bank to the new government of the United States. They used the local farmers and their teams and wagons to haul goods giving the farmers some much needed extra income. These farmers were not paid in cash, but were given a Portage Account Credit for the loads carried by them. These credits were redeemable at any of the stores operated by the principals in the Portage Road Company.

James Thompson of Whirlpool Farm built up enough credit that he only had to pay eighteen shillings and one pence on purchases of forty pounds, sixteen shillings and one pence over the course of a year. His total credit was forty-one pounds, four shillings and six pence with two pounds, sixteen shillings and six pence deducted for road maintenance.

Robert Hamilton owned wharf and warehouse complexes at Queenston, Chippawa and Fort Erie, which made him one of the richest men in Upper Canada. Hamilton died in 1809 leaving his sons to run the family affairs. The extent of the traffic over the portage can be seen in this account by a traveler, J.C. Ogden, in 1799: "At the Lower Landing, Queenston, the vessels discharge their cargoes, and take on furs brought from three hundred to fifteen hundred miles back. I have seen four vessels of sixty to one hundred tons unloading at once and sixty wagons loaded in a day for the Upper Landing at Chippawa."

The Portage Road began a steep climb up the escarpment as soon as it left the village of Queenston. It ambled through Stamford Township where the drivers could stop for refreshments at several taverns along the way. One of the first was the Whirlpool Inn, owned by Andrew Rorbach, at the corner of the Portage Road and Church's Lane. Rorbach was also a saddler and drivers could have a drink and broken harnesses repaired at the same time.

An inn was also built at the crossroads of the Portage Road and Lundy's Lane. This crossroad, which eventually became part of the city of Niagara Falls was described by a visitor this way: "On the part of the road leading to Lake Erie which draws nearest the falls, there is a small village consisting of about half a dozen straggling houses; here we alighted and having disposed of our horses, made a slight repast."

Less than a mile from the Crossroads stood another tavern run by James Forsyth who worked a farm on 388 acres in the area. This tavern sat just south of present day Symmes Street in Niagara Falls. Yet another tavern operated by Charles Wilson stood at Fallsview where the Minolta Tower Centre is located today. There were many other taverns scattered along the Portage Road all the way to Chippawa.

Chippawa, the southern terminus of the Portage Road, was also a bustling community, although it never reached the status of Queenston. It boasted a number of inns through the early part of the nineteenth century. There were two in 1796, the Fairbanks House and John Fanning's Hotel. An interesting anecdote from George Holley, who visited the area in 1796 will be familiar to many modern air travelers. He took the stage from Queenston to Chippawa along the Portage Road. After dining at Fanning's he: "found our goods (bags) were not in Chippawa, and was obliged to go to Queenston after them - as I could not get a horse, was obliged to walk."

In 1800 James Macklem opened a new tavern in Chippawa. In 1807 he entered in partnership with John Fanning and Benjamin Hardison of Fort Erie to build a mill at the head of the rapids of the Niagara. This enterprise only ran for a few years when it burned down in February of 1812.

In 1808 a traveler known only as T.C. left us this account of the accommodations in Chippawa: ". . . Chippewa(sic) there are two good taverns; one kept by Stevens and the other by Fanning . . . Each has a new part connected with old buildings and each has eight windows in front. The dining-room at Stevens' is twenty by thirty feet, carpeted. The attendance is good and the people civil. For a pint of tolerable Tenerife, a gill of rum, supper, breakfast, bed, and feed for my horse, I paid thirteen shillings and six pence, York money."

In the southern part of the peninsula, Fort Erie had a regular ferry service to Black Rock and Buffalo as well as the military post. Several merchants had warehouses located here to facilitate trade with the upper lakes. There were also settlements to the west of Fort Erie notably Stone Bridge and the Sugar Loaf, which served the rural communities of Humberstone, Crowland and Wainfleet Townships.

The peace and tranquility, so apparent as the second decade of the nineteenth century progressed, was soon to be shattered. The War of 1812 was close at hand.

HISTORICAL NOTES: The community of Lawrenceville became known as Virgil in the latter part of the 19th century.

CHAPTER TWENTY-FOUR
<u>A PIONEER CHRISTMAS</u>

When William Hamilton Merritt made his way from Queenston to his parents home near Shipman's Corners on the Twelve Mile Creek in December of 1809, after riding all the way from Albany, New York, the thing that would be uppermost in his mind was Christmas. He would be home for Christmas!

Whether in the thriving metropolis of Niagara or in the fledgling communities like Shipman's Corners or Stone Bridge, Christmas was a season for family and friends. For one day the drudgery and battle for survival were forgotten in a burst of goodwill and rejoicing.

When the pioneers first came to the Peninsula their celebration of Christmas was quite different from the way we celebrate today. In the 1790's it was a religious feast as the customs that mark our celebrations had not yet made an appearance in Upper Canada.

The day might begin with the chores quickly being attended to before going to church, if they were lucky enough to be near one. Often a simple prayer service with a few neighbours followed by the best feast the farm could supply for family and friends was the order of the day. A pig or some barnyard fowl was fattened for the occasion with, perhaps, some venison to supplement the simple fare.

The secular aspects of Christmas were not a factor until much later. The first mention of Christmas in Niagara newspapers was not until 1826 when the Farmer's Journal published a short poem. Three years later the editor remarked: "If we did not turn to the calendar occasionally for the day of the month, the beautiful festoons of evergreens which decorate the walls and windows of many of our churches would admonish us that the revolving year has once more brought us to the threshold of that memorable day which is celebrated, by a large portion of the Christian Church, as the anniversary of the Messiah's birth and set apart as a cheerful festival throughout the whole of Christendom."

One custom that was followed was that of the Yule Log. This was a large log that served as the foundation for the fire in the hearth throughout the Christmas season.

The Yule Log was usually obtained on Christmas eve and one pioneer left us this description of the event: "Suddenly a great roar shook the woods and the swift mounting crackle of the flames topped the tallest tree. They were burning the branches from the yule log. Jack says it's bad luck to wait. There is luck, he says, in a yule log that lasts twelve days."

The great fire roared and crackled. The women at the window could see black shadows mingling and moving about the fire. Jack, his children and his men joined hands and danced about the fire. Then the log was cant hooked into chains and onto a stoneboat (a sleigh used to remove stones from a field) for the journey to the house. The children heaped snow on the embers until they were out as the men dragged their burden home.

Amid excited shouts the door flew open and the yule log was dragged and carried to the hearth. For once the woman of the house did not mind the mess of bark and black streaks on her floor. With much sweating and heaving the log was canted into place up against the back of the fireplace. Dry pine logs flanked it and dry strips of cedar lay before it. Jack, a flaming pitch pine root in his hand, with grace and ceremony, set the Christmas fire blazing.

The first recorded Yule Log in the peninsula was in 1790 at a Christmas wedding. An eye witness described it like this: "The bare little log house was gay with spruce boughs and sprays of red rowan berries, and the ceremony took place where the dancing light of the yule log lighted the faces of the bride and groom."

This was another custom that seemed to be prevalent in the early days, Christmas was considered an excellent time for a wedding. Perhaps it was the one time when everyone could gather for such a happy occasion.

In the 1830s the celebration of Christmas

began to change. A revival of the Christmas carol, out of favour since the days of the Puritans, started at this time. However, many of the carols we sing today had not yet made an appearance. "Silent Night", written in German in 1818, was not translated into English until 1843. "We Three Kings of Orient Are" was set to music in 1857 and "O Little Town of Bethlehem" was not written until 1865. One of the best loved hymns of Christmas, "O Come All Ye Faithful", was written in the thirteenth century but not translated into English until 1841.

In the late 1830s it became fashionable to hitch up the horse and go for a sleigh ride on Christmas Day. There are records of people sleighing on the ice bridge below Niagara Falls in 1839.

It was about this time that people began to decorate their homes with evergreen boughs and the like, although the Christmas tree had not yet become common. The Christmas tree was a German tradition and many settlers of German descent followed it. However, it was not until 1841, when Prince Albert, the husband of Queen Victoria, erected one at Windsor Castle that it took hold among the English people and eventually made its way to Upper Canada.

The tree was decorated with small coloured candles held on to the branches by tin holders. The tree also contained hand made ornaments and the lighter gifts in the branches. The heavier gifts were placed under the tree as we do today.

Christmas was a day of fun and thanksgiving for our pioneer forbearers and this Christmas let us remember the sacrifices that they made to pass on to us this place we call home.

May your holidays be merry and your New Year be filled with the luck of the Yule Log.

CHAPTER TWENTY-FIVE

THE EVE OF WAR

For thousands of years the Niagara Peninsula had been a home of abundance for aboriginal peoples who came to hunt and fish in its woods and streams. The Neutrals settled here in the fourteenth century and thrived in a unique setting as farmer, trader and warrior. After the scattering of that tribe in 1652 the peninsula lay in quiet contemplation until the coming of the loyalists some one hundred and thirty years later.

By 1812 thirty years had passed since the first settlers crossed the Niagara at Queenston to wrest a living from the virgin forests of the Niagara Peninsula. Many brought their families from great distance by wagons pulled by teams of oxen through days of wilderness and danger to start over in a new land. They could be proud of their achievements in such a short time. Land was cleared, seeds sown and the land tamed and groomed to bring forth the myriad crops not seen since the days of the Neutrals.

Settlements sprang up with their inevitable industries and services to cater to the growing population. The little community of Shipman's Corners on the Twelve Mile Creek boasted an interdenominational church, a tavern, a school and several stores and mills. It fast became a centre for the farmers along the creek who used the mills and mercantiles for their source of supplies and the processing of their crops.

Niagara was the military and legal centre of the part of Upper Canada west of Kingston even though the capital had been moved to that backwater, aptly named, Muddy York,. The capital had yet to reach its potential as a social and commerial centre.

The Portage Road was a busy commercial highway with businesses growing up along its route. It was anchored at either end by the village of Chippawa in the south and the commercial centre of the area, Queenston, in the north.

At the other end of the peninsula things were progressing as well. Fort Erie's wharfs and warehouses bulged with the merchandise of the fur trade. A thriving community grew up around the Sugar Loaf with a grist mill, flax seed mill and a saw mill in full operation. Just north of the Sugar loaf was the village of Stonebridge with its blacksmith shop, merchants, harness maker, tailor and many of the other amenities of a growing community. Over one hundred families called this part of the peninsula home.

Peace reigned supreme on the frontier. Commerce between the peninsula and the Americans from Fort Niagara to Buffalo was profitable and amiable. Friendships flourished across the waters of the Niagara. Goods and livestock regularly passed from one shore to the other on the many ferries servicing the area.

However, dark clouds began to appear on the horizon. Events in far away places were conspiring to disrupt the lives of the peninsula pioneers.

In 1807 Great Britain, entangled in a bitter war with Napoleonic France, passed the Orders-in-Council reserving the right to stop any neutral ship on the high seas to prevent them from trading with occupied Europe. American ships were seized with regularity much to the chagrin of the American authorities. Protests fell on deaf ears and the threat of war ebbed and flowed as one crisis followed another.

Stopping and searching American ships was bad enough, but, another practice of the captains of British warships, which rankled the Americans even more was the impressment of American sailors into the British Navy. Many British sailors were "pressed", that is, seized and put on board British man-of-wars to serve for the duration. Today we would call it conscription.

American ships, stopped on the high seas, were searched for British citizens who were considered fair game by the perennially short handed captains. Sometimes highhanded captains rejected the papers of American citizens and pressed them as well even from American warships.

On a cold February day in 1807 the British Frigate "Melampus" lay anchored in Hampton

Roads, Chesapeake Bay, Virginia. The captain was entertaining local dignitaries and fellow officers when three American seamen, impressed on the high seas, precipitated an incident that led to the brink of war. Daniel Martin, a Negro from Massachusetts, William Ware, an Indian from Maryland and John Strachan also of Maryland saw the captain's gig in the water and made good their escape.

The trio immediately signed on with the American Frigate "Chesapeake" which set sail shortly afterward. The three deserters made the mistake of thumbing their nose at the Melampus on the way by. The British gave chase and, after a ten minute cannonade, boarded the battered Chesapeake and recovered the three plus a British deserter whom they later hanged at Halifax with much sabre rattling and denunciations from the American press. The crisis, however, passed.

In the meantime, a little closer to home, the Americans were sowing the seeds of a bitter enemy. In the Indiana Territory the governor, William Henry Harrison, was hungry for land. He was pushing the western Indians out of their traditional hunting grounds, buying land worth two dollars an acre for a fraction of the price. The Shawnee resisted.

On November 6, 1811 Harrison attacked the Indians at Tippecanoe destroying the Indian community of Prophet's Town and making a mortal enemy of the man who would rally the western tribes to the British cause in the coming war. That enemy was the Shawnee Chief, Techumseh.

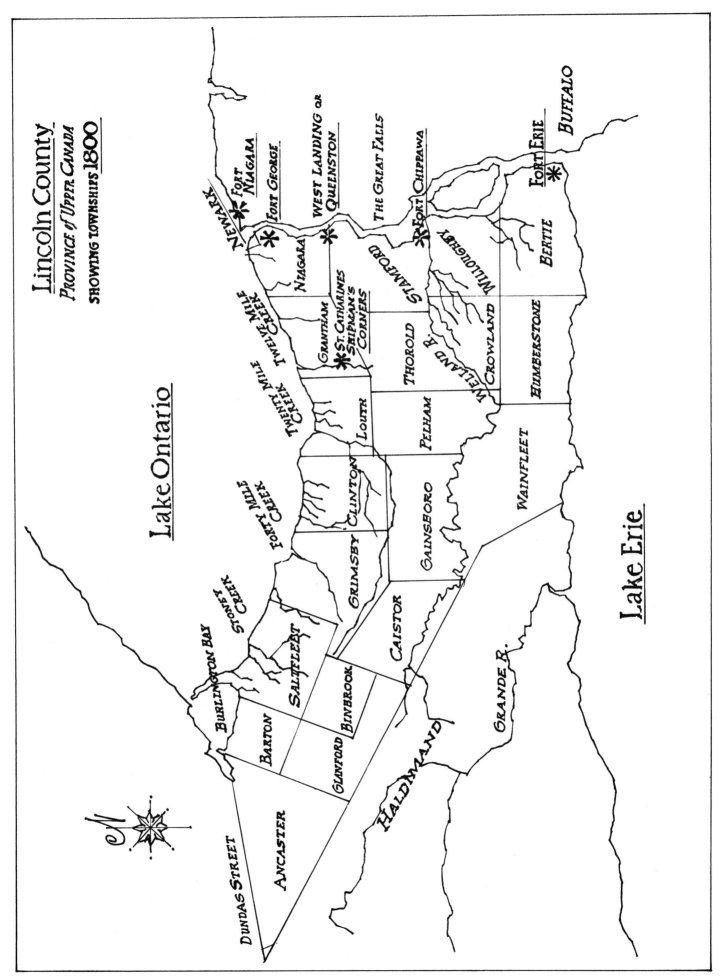

Lincoln County

Province of Upper Canada

SHOWING TOWNSHIPS 1800

Lake Ontario

Lake Erie

DUNDAS STREET

BURLINGTON BAY

STONEY CREEK

FORTY MILE CREEK

BARTON

SALTFLEET

GLANFORD

BINBROOK

ANCASTER

GRIMSBY

CLINTON

LOUTH

CAISTOR

GAINSBORO

HALDIMAND

GRANDE R.

WAINFLEET

PELHAM

GRANTHAM

ST. CATHARINES
SHIPMAN'S CORNERS

THOROLD

WELLAND R.

CROWLAND

HUMBERSTONE

TWELVE MILE CREEK

TWENTY MILE CREEK

NEWARK

NIAGARA

FORT NIAGARA

FORT GEORGE

WEST LANDING OR QUEENSTON

THE GREAT FALLS

STAMFORD

FORT CHIPPAWA

WILLOUGHBY

BERTIE

FORT ERIE

BUFFALO

N